TCP/IP JumpStart

TCP/IP JumpStart™

Andrew G. Blank

SYBEX®

San Francisco ◆ Paris ◆ Düsseldorf ◆ Soest ◆ London

Associate Publisher: Neil Edde

Contracts and Licensing Manager: Kristine O'Callaghan

Acquisitions & Developmental Editor: Linda Lee

Editor: Sharon Wilkey

Project Editors: Chad Mack, Colleen Wheeler Strand

Technical Editor: Robert Gradante

Book Designer: Maureen Forys, Happenstance Type-O-Rama

Graphic Illustrator: Jerry Williams!

Electronic Publishing Specialist: Maureen Forys, Happenstance Type-O-Rama

Project Team Leader: Leslie Higbee

Proofreaders: Molly Glover, Jennifer Campbell

Indexer: Nancy Guenther

Cover Designer: Archer Design

Cover Illustrator/Photographer: Archer Design

Library of Congress Card Number: 99-69459

ISBN: 0-7821-2644-8

Manufactured in the United States of America

10 9 8 7 6 5 4 3 2 1

To my inspiration, my encourager, my perfect match, my best friend, and the love of my life, my wife Suzie; you have had a profound and awesome impact on my life. I love you very much.

To my son A.J. and my daughter Amber, I treasure your love and have tremendous pride in both of you; Daddy loves you so much.

Making the Most of This Book

At the beginning of each chapter of *TCP/IP JumpStart*, you'll find a list of topics that you can expect to learn about within that chapter. As you read through the chapter, you'll notice that when a topic continues to the next page, you'll see this icon at the bottom outside corner of the page:

When a topic ends, you'll see this icon:

To help you soak up new material easily, I've highlighted **new terms** in bold and defined them in the margins of the pages. And to give you some hands-on experience, there are Test It Out sections that let you practice what you've just learned. In addition, several special elements highlight important information:

NOTE

Notes provide extra information and references to related information.

TIP

Tips are insights that help you perform tasks more easily and effectively.

WARNING

Warnings let you know about things you should do—or shouldn't do—as you learn more about TCP/IP.

At the end of each chapter, you can test your knowledge of the topics covered by answering the chapter's Review Questions. (You'll find the answers to the Review Questions in Appendix A.)

There's also some special material for your reference. If you'd like to quickly look up the meaning of a term, Appendix B is a glossary of terms that have been introduced throughout the book. If you are wondering what acronyms stand for, Appendix C is an acronym guide showing the acronyms in this book spelled out. Because TCP/IP is a current technology and is likely to constantly change, a Web site has been set up to accompany this book. Appendix D describes the materials that you will find on the *TCP/IP JumpStart* companion Web site.

Chapter

1

The Origin of TCP/IP and the Internet

Two people can communicate effectively when they agree to use a common language. They could speak English, Spanish, French, or even sign language, but they must use the same language.

Computers work the same way. Transmission Control Protocol/Internet Protocol (TCP/IP) is like a language that computers speak. More specifically, TCP/IP is a set of rules that defines how two computers address each other and send data to each other. This set of rules is called a protocol. Multiple protocols that are grouped together form a protocol suite and work together as a protocol stack.

TCP/IP is a strong, fast, scalable, and efficient suite of protocols. This protocol stack is the de facto protocol of the Internet. As information exchange via the Internet becomes more widespread, more individuals and companies will need to understand TCP/IP.

In this first chapter you'll look at the origins of TCP/IP. You will learn about:

   The features of TCP/IP

   ARPAnet

   TCP's method of moving data

   Requests for Comments (RFCs)

   The benefits of using TCP/IP

What Is TCP/IP?

TCP/IP is a set of **protocols** that enable communication between computers. There was a time when it was not important for computers to communicate with each other. There was no need for a common protocol. But as computers became networked, the need arose for computers to agree on certain protocols.

protocols
Rules or standards that govern communications.

network administrator
A person who installs, monitors, and troubleshoots a network.

Today, a **network administrator** can choose from many protocols, but the TCP/IP protocol is the most widely used. Part of the reason is that TCP/IP is the protocol of choice on the Internet—the world's largest network. If you want a computer to communicate on the Internet, it'll have to use TCP/IP.

NOTE

When multiple protocols work together, the group is collectively known as a protocol suite or protocol stack. TCP/IP is an example of a protocol suite (it describes multiple protocols that work together). The implementation of TCP/IP is described as a protocol stack. Both terms are used interchangeably, yet their definitions vary slightly.

Another reason for TCP/IP's popularity is that it is compatible with almost every computer in the world. The TCP/IP stack is supported by current versions of all the major operating systems and network operating systems—including Windows 95/98, Windows NT, Windows 2000, Linux, Unix, and NetWare.

Unlike proprietary protocols developed by hardware and software vendors to make their equipment work, TCP/IP enjoys support from a variety of hardware and software vendors. Examples of companies that have products that work with TCP/IP include Microsoft, Novell, IBM, Apple, and Red Hat. Many other companies also support the TCP/IP protocol suite.

TCP/IP is sometimes referred to as "the language of the Internet." In addition to being the official language of the Internet, TCP/IP is also the official language of many smaller networks. For all the computers that are attached to the Internet to communicate effectively, they must agree on a language. Just like every human language has certain rules so that the people involved in the conversation understand what the other is saying, a computer language needs a set of rules so that computers can effectively communicate. Some of the rules of a language that computers use to communicate include determining when to send data and when to receive data.

Features of TCP/IP

TCP/IP has been in a use for more than 20 years, and time has proven it to be a tested and stable protocol suite. TCP/IP has many features and benefits. In this section, you will learn about some of the most important ones.

Support from Vendors

As stated earlier, TCP/IP receives support from many hardware and software vendors. This means that the TCP/IP suite is not tied to the development efforts of a single company. Instead, the choice to use TCP/IP on a network can be based on the purpose of the network and not on the hardware or software that has been purchased.

Interoperability

One of the major reasons why the TCP/IP suite has gained popularity and acceptance so universally is that it can be installed and used on virtually every platform. For example, using TCP/IP, a Unix host can communicate and transfer data to a DOS host or a Windows host. A **host** is another name for a computer or device on a network. TCP/IP eliminates the cross-platform boundaries.

Flexibility

TCP/IP is an extremely flexible protocol suite, and in later chapters you will learn about some features that contribute to this flexibility. Examples of TCP/IP's flexibility include the latitude an administrator has in assigning and reassigning addresses. An administrator can automatically or manually assign an IP address to a host, and a TCP/IP host can convert easy-to-remember names, such as www.sybex.com, to a TCP/IP address.

Routability

A limitation of many protocols is their difficulty moving data from one segment of the network to another. TCP/IP is exceptionally well adapted to the process of routing data from one segment of the network to another, or from a host on a network in one part of the world to a host on a network in another part of the world.

In the following sections, you will learn about how these features of TCP/IP grew out of the military's need for a reliable, flexible networking standard.

host
Any device (such as a workstation, server, mainframe, or printer) on a network or internetwork that has a TCP/IP address.

3

The Origins of the Internet: ARPAnet

ARPAnet

The Advanced Research Projects Agency's supernetwork–the predecessor of the Internet.

Network Control Protocol (NCP)

The protocol used before TCP/IP.

Understanding the roots of the Internet will give you insight into the development of TCP/IP and many of its rules and standards. If you know why TCP/IP was created and how it evolved, the TCP/IP protocol suite is easier to understand.

The predecessor of today's Internet was **ARPAnet**, a supernetwork that was created by the Advanced Research Projects Agency (ARPA) and launched in 1969. This network was created in response to the potential threat of nuclear attack from the Soviet Union. One of ARPA's primary goals was to design a fault-tolerant network that would enable U.S. military leaders to stay in contact in case of nuclear war. By the standards of the time, this fault-tolerant network seemed to be almost science fiction. ARPA set out on a mission to create a network with what seemed to be impossible requirements.

NOTE

In the late 1950s, the United States Department of Defense (DoD), under the guidance of one of America's leading think tanks, the RAND corporation, formed the Advanced Research Projects Agency (ARPA).

The protocol, or language of choice, used on the ARPAnet was called **Network Control Protocol (NCP)**–TCP/IP had not yet been developed. As the ARPAnet grew, however, a new protocol was needed because NCP simply didn't fulfill all the needs of a larger network. The NCP protocol was similar to a human language that has only a few words. The language might enable a few people to communicate, but as you include more people who want to talk about many more subjects, you have to improve the language.

The ARPAnet project had some specific goals and requirements. To reach these goals and meet these requirements, some of the top computer minds worked in a collaborative effort with little financial or public glory. Many of the top computer minds that worked on the ARPAnet were affiliated with major universities. It was not the intention of the project leaders to create the worldwide network that exists today, but fantastic growth soon followed the ARPAnet's humble beginnings.

ARPAnet's Requirements

To fulfill the needs of the military, the new ARPAnet had to meet the following requirements:

No one point more critical than any other   Because the network needed to be able to withstand a nuclear war, there could be no one critical part of the network and no single point of failure. If there were any critical parts of the network, enemies could target that area and eliminate communications.

Redundant routes to any destination   Because any location on the network could be taken down by enemies in the event of a war, there had to be multiple routes from any source to any destination on the network. Without redundant routes, any one location could become a critical communications link and a potential point of failure.

On-the-fly rerouting of data   If any part of the network failed, the network had to be able to reroute data to its destination on-the-fly.

Ability to connect different types of computers over different types of networks   This network could not be tied to just one operating system or hardware type. Because universities, government agencies, and corporations often rely on different types of Local Area Networks (LANs) and network operating systems, interoperability among these many networks was critical. Connecting to the network should not dictate that a lot of new hardware had to be purchased; rather, the existing hardware should suffice.

Not controlled by a single corporation   If one corporation had a monopoly on this network, the network would grow to boost the corporation instead of the usefulness and effectiveness of the network. This network needed to be a cooperative effort among many engineers who were working to improve the network for the sake of the supernetwork, not that of a corporation.

By December of 1969 the ARPAnet had four hosts. The ARPAnet consisted of computers at the University of California at Los Angeles, the University of California at Santa Barbara, the University of Utah, and Stanford Research Institute. The ARPAnet set the foundation for what would grow up to be the Internet.

Requests for Comments

To improve the technology that was being used on the ARPAnet, a system was designed to encourage and facilitate correspondence among the engineers who were developing this new network. This system, which is still in use today, relies on **Requests for Comments (RFCs)** to provide feedback and collaboration among engineers. An RFC is a paper that has been written by an engineer, a team of engineers, or just someone with a better idea, to define a new technology or enhance an existing technology.

The process of submitting RFCs was designed to be a "bulletin board" for posting technical theories. The old-school way of writing a thesis or book was too slow. RFCs provided an informal and fast way to share new technologies and ideas for enhancements. After an RFC is written and posted, it can be evaluated, critiqued, and used by other engineers and developers. If another engineer or developer can improve on the theory or standard, the RFC provides an open forum in which to do so. Many of these papers are long, painstakingly technical, and in most cases good reading material for someone with difficulty sleeping.

An RFC can be submitted for review to the **Internet Engineering Task Force (IETF)**. Engineers from the IETF review the papers that are submitted and assign a number to each. From that point on, the RFC number becomes the effective "name" of the paper. For example, the first RFC, which is about host software, is called RFC 1. RFC 1 was submitted in 1969 by a developer named Steve Crocker. There are currently more than 2,000 RFCs.

As the ARPAnet was growing and researchers and engineers were making improvements, they used RFCs as a tool to strengthen and ensure the network's foundation. TCP/IP is a child of the RFC method of development—no corporation makes money when you install TCP/IP. Using RFCs has been the method of growing the ARPAnet with the best network minds contributing.

Request For Comment (RFC)
A paper thoroughly describing a new protocol or technology.

Internet Engineering Task Force (IETF)
A governing body of the Internet.

TIP

It is possible for anyone to write and publish an RFC. Instructions on how to write and submit an RFC are detailed in RFC 2223. Today, RFCs are posted on many Web sites. Appendix D describes this book's companion Web site, which has links to RFC 2223 and other RFC Web sites.

The Birth of TCP/IP

As stated earlier, the "language" spoken by hosts on the ARPAnet in 1969 was called NCP. However, NCP had too many limitations and was not robust enough for the supernetwork, which was beginning to grow out of control. The limitations of NCP and the growth of the ARPAnet lead to research and development of a new network language.

In 1974 Vint Cerf and Bob Kahn, two Internet pioneers, published "A Protocol for Packet Network Interconnection." This paper describes the **Transmission Control Protocol (TCP)**, which is a protocol in the protocol suite that would eventually replace NCP.

The TCP protocol describes the host-to-host portion of a communication. TCP explains how two hosts can set up this communication and how they can stay in touch with each other as data is being transferred. NCP did not resolve these issues to the extent that TCP was able to.

As you will learn in later chapters, TCP is responsible for making sure that the data gets through to the other host. It keeps track of what is sent and retransmits anything that did not get through. If any message is too large for one package, TCP splits the message into several packages and makes sure that they all arrive correctly. After they have arrived, TCP at the other end puts all the packages back together in the proper order.

By 1978, testing and further development of this language led to a new suite of protocols called **Transmission Control Protocol/Internet Protocol (TCP/IP)**. In 1982, it was decided that TCP/IP would replace NCP as the standard language of the ARPAnet. RFC 801 describes how and why the transition from NCP to TCP was to take place. On January 1, 1983, ARPAnet switched over to TCP/IP and the network continued to grow exponentially.

In 1990, the ARPAnet ceased to exist. The Internet has since grown from ARPAnet's roots, and TCP/IP has evolved to meet the changing requirements of the Internet.

Transmission Control Protocol (TCP)
The protocol describing communication between hosts.

Transmission Control Protocol/ Internet Protocol (TCP/IP)
The suite of protocols that when combined create the "language of the Internet."

Design Goals of TCP/IP

TCP/IP has evolved to its current state. The protocols within the TCP/IP suite have been tested, modified, and improved over time. The original TCP/IP protocol suite had several design goals that intended to make it a viable protocol for the large, evolving internetwork. Some of these goals included:

Hardware independence   A protocol suite that could be used on a Mac, PC, mainframe, or any other computer.

Software independence   A protocol suite that could be used by different software vendors and applications. This would enable a host on one site to communicate with a host on another site, without having the same software configuration.

Failure recovery and the ability to handle high error rates   A protocol suite that featured automatic recovery from any dropped or lost data. This protocol must be able to recover from an outage of any host on any part of the network and at any point in a data transfer.

Efficient protocol with low overhead   A protocol suite that had a minimal amount of "extra" data moving with the data being transferred. This extra data, called overhead, functions as packaging for the data being transferred and enables the data transmission. Overhead is similar to an envelope used to send a letter, or a box used to send a bigger item—having too much overhead is as efficient as using a large crate to send someone a necklace.

Ability to add new networks to the internetwork without service disruption   A protocol suite that enabled new, independent networks to join this network of networks without bringing down the larger internetwork.

Routable Data   A protocol suite on which data could make its way through an internetwork of computers to any possible destination. For this to be possible, a single and meaningful addressing scheme must be used so that every computer that is moving the data can compute the best path of every piece of data as it moves through the network.

The TCP/IP protocol suite has evolved to meet these goals. Throughout this book, you will learn how TCP/IP has met and surpassed these original design goals.

Moving Data across the Network

Creating this new "super network" introduced many new concepts and challenges for the pioneering engineers. One of the most critical issues was how to move data across the network. Older communications protocols relied on a circuit-switched technology. TCP/IP, however, introduced a new way of moving data across a network. The protocol suite set a new standard for communications and data transport by using a packet-switched network.

TCP/IP's method of moving data and information helped the protocol suite fulfill several of the requirements for the growing ARPAnet supernetwork. In the following sections, you'll learn about how circuit-switched and packet-switched communications methods work.

circuit-switched network
A network on which all data in a communication takes the same path.

Moving Data on a Circuit-Switched Network

Historically, data has moved through a **circuit-switched network**. In a circuit-switched network, data moves across the same path throughout the entire communication. An example of a circuit-switched network is the telephone system. When you make a telephone call, a single path (also called a circuit) is established between the caller and the recipient. For the rest of the conversation, the voice data keeps moving through the same circuit. If you were to make a call and get a very staticky connection, you would hang up and try again. This way you could get a different circuit, hopefully one with less static. Early network data transmissions followed this type of pathway.

In the illustration below, notice that although the data could take multiple routes, all the data moves from the source to the destination along the same path. In a circuit-switched network, data communication moves along a single, established route.

Moving Data on a Packet-Switched Network

A circuit-switched network was unacceptable for both the ARPAnet and the Internet. Data had to be able to move through different routes so that if one circuit went down or got staticky, it didn't affect communication on the rest of the network. Instead, data simply would take a different route.

The Internet uses a **packet-switched network**. On a packet-switched network, the computer that is sending the data fragments the data into smaller, more manageable chunks. These chunks are called **packets**. Each packet is then individually addressed and sent to its intended recipient. As the several packets make their way through the network, each packet finds its own way to the receiver. The receiving computer reassembles the packets into the original message.

The illustration below shows how TCP/IP moves data. Notice that there are several routes that the data packets can follow from the source to the destination. Unlike the illustration on the preceding page, the data packets here use a variety of routes—some follow the same path, while others follow different paths. Each packet follows its own route, and data is reassembled at the destination. This is how information moves on a packet-switched network.

packet-switched network
A network on which the data in a communication takes several paths.

packet
A unit of data that is prepared for transmission onto a network.

R= Router
D= Data

Source

Destination

Understanding How a Packet-Switched Network Functions

To help you understand how a packet-switched network moves data, let's look at a similar real-world situation.

Let's say that I take my son's soccer team to an arcade and restaurant for a team party. I have the whole team outside of the arcade. My task is to get the team to the other side of the arcade, to my wife who is waiting for them in the restaurant. In this analogy, the team represents the complete file on one host, and each child represents a data packet. One of my goals is to lose as few of the kids as possible.

While we are standing outside, it is easy to put the team in order; all the children are wearing numbered jerseys. I tell the kids that we will meet on the other side of the arcade in a restaurant for pizza and that they should all move as fast as possible through the arcade and to the restaurant.

After I open the door and say, "go," the kids enter one at a time. Entering the arcade one at a time represents the fragmenting and sending of the file. Just as each of the kids has a numbered jersey, each packet has a number so that the receiving host can put the data back together.

Now picture a dozen six-year-olds moving through the arcade. Some of the children will take a short route; others will take a long route. Possibly, they'll all take the same route, though it is much more likely that they will all take different routes. Some will get hung up at certain spots, but others will move through faster. My wife is in the restaurant waiting to receive the team. As they start arriving at the restaurant, she can reassemble the children (packets) in the correct order because they all have a number on their backs. If any are missing, she will wait just a bit for the stragglers and then send back a message that she is missing part of the team (file).

After I receive a message that she is missing a child (a packet), I can resend the missing part. I do not need to resend the entire team (all the packets), just the missing child (packet or packets).

Please note, however, I would not go look for the lost child, I would just put the same numbered jersey on a clone of the lost child and send him into the arcade to find the restaurant.

Why Use TCP/IP?

TCP/IP offers many advantages over other network protocols and protocol suites. Here is a summary of some of the benefits of using the TCP/IP protocol suite:

internetwork
Several smaller networks connected together.

Widely published, open standard   TCP/IP is not a secret. It is not proprietary or owned by any corporation. Because it is a published protocol with no secrets, any computer engineer is able to improve or enhance the protocol by publishing an RFC.

Compatible with different computer systems   TCP/IP enables any system to communicate with any other system. It is like a universal language that would enable people from any country to communicate effectively with people from any other country.

Works on different hardware and network configurations   TCP/IP is accepted and can be configured for virtually every network created.

Routable protocol   TCP/IP can figure out the path of every piece of data as it moves through the network. Because TCP/IP is a routable protocol, the size of any TCP/IP network is virtually unlimited.

Reliable, efficient data delivery   TCP/IP can guarantee that the data is transferred to another host.

Single addressing scheme   TCP/IP uses a single and relatively simple addressing scheme. You will learn about TCP/IP's addressing in Chapter 6. An administrator can transfer knowledge of TCP/IP to any TCP/IP network without relearning the addressing scheme.

The Internet has become a necessity for business, and it soon will be a necessity at home. Many businesses, large and small, are connected to the Internet and are using TCP/IP as the protocol of choice for their internal networks. As more and more homes connect to the Internet, those computers will also use the TCP/IP protocol suite. The commercial implications of the Internet have changed the dynamic of every business model that has ever been taught.

The Origin of TCP/IP and the Internet

TCP/IP is the standard for a communications protocol on the Internet. You cannot connect to the Internet without using TCP/IP. Whether you build a network at home with two hosts or you manage an **internetwork** at your business with 100,000 hosts, TCP/IP is a communications protocol that will work effectively. TCP/IP can scale to any size environment and is robust enough to connect different types of LANs.

These are a few of the many reasons why network administrators choose to use TCP/IP as the protocol on their networks.

Review Questions

Terms to Know

❑ protocols
❑ network administrator
❑ host
❑ ARPAnet
❑ NCP
❑ RFC
❑ IETF
❑ TCP
❑ TCP/IP
❑ circuit-switched network
❑ packet-switched network
❑ packet
❑ internetwork

1. The Internet was originally called:

_____

2. List three requirements that the military mandated of this new network.

_____

_____

_____

3. Another name for a computer on a TCP/IP network is:

_____

4. Describe packet-switched and circuit-switched networks.

_____

5. What is an RFC?

_____

6. What protocol did TCP/IP replace?

_____

7. True or False: TCP/IP is one protocol.

_____

8. What is IETF?

_____

What Are Protocols?

A protocol is a rule or a set of rules and standards for communicating that computers use when they send data back and forth. Both the sender and receiver involved in data transfer must recognize and observe the same protocols.

To exchange data, the sending and the receiving computers, also called hosts, must agree on what the data will look like. When one host is sending another host a whole bunch of 1s and 0s, both hosts have to agree on the meaning and placement of each 1 and each 0. Part of the information that is sent represents addresses and part is data—each host has a unique address, just as you have a unique address on your street. And just like a letter being delivered to your address, data is delivered to the appropriate host based on its address. The hosts that send the information must understand how to find the correct address among the data so that the data can be routed to its destination.

When hosts begin communicating with each other, they first must agree on what protocols to use. This is similar to two people who are going to have a conversation: They have to agree on which language to use and what the rules for the conversation will be. They must agree on who will talk first, how to address the other, how to acknowledge that the information is understood, and how to finish or close the conversation. In the following illustration, Harry the Host is trying to set up communication with another host. The first thing that they need to agree on is the language, or protocols, to use.

Harry   Gary

9. List four benefits of using TCP/IP.

_____

_____

_____

_____

10. What year was the change made from NCP to TCP/IP?

_____

Chapter

2

Protocols

In the first chapter, you learned how the
ARPAnet and how TCP/IP was develope
work industry has grown, rules and stan
rules and standards have formed the TCP/IP
and robust standard used by computers to c
examines why protocols are important and
nication between hosts.

In this chapter you will learn about:

 Protocols

 Packets

 The seven layers of the OSI model

 The four layers of the DoD model

Protocols

A group of protocols is called a **protocol suite** or a **protocol stack**. A single protocol addresses one particular issue that helps to enable communication—for example, defining what an address looks like. When combined with other protocols, the protocol group that results is called a protocol suite. TCP/IP, for example, is a protocol suite. At a computer that is communicating on a network, the software that packages the data and prepares it for transmission is called a protocol stack. When a computer is receiving data, the data moves up through the protocol stack.

Protocol suites are typically referred to by just a couple of the protocols in the suite. Rather than refer to a suite by a name that might include as many as 20 protocols, you can simply reference it by an easier-to-use and more friendly name. Many protocol suites are in use today. Some are proprietary protocols that have limited use. These are developed for specific purposes to meet some particular need of the hardware or software involved.

Some of the popular protocol suites in today's network communications include:

IPX/SPX   This is the protocol suite that Novell has implemented with its operating system. The acronym stands for Internetwork Packet Exchange/Sequenced Packet Exchange.

AppleTalk   This is the protocol suite that Apple has implemented with its operating system.

TCP/IP   This is the protocol suite that has been made a standard of the Internet. Anyone who would like to use the Internet must use the TCP/IP suite.

Some of the questions that a protocol might answer include:

◆ What type of cable or transmission media is used to connect hosts on the network?

◆ How is data transmitted on the transmission media?

◆ How do the hosts on the network know when to transmit data?

◆ How does each host know how much data can be transmitted at a time?

◆ How can hosts using different operating systems communicate?

◆ How can a host check the data received for transmissions?

protocol suite
A combination of protocols.

protocol stack
Protocols that send and receive data.

19

Protocols Move Packets of Data

When data is sent from one host to another, the Transmission Control Protocol of TCP/IP divides the data into more manageable "chunks." As explained in Chapter 1, these chunks are called packets. The protocol determines how the packets are formed and addressed—the packets are like crates that are used to ship the data.

Each of the packets has a set of **headers** applied to it. The headers usually include addressing and routing information, which makes it possible to reassemble the packets and have the original data at the destination. The headers are applied to the packets for the same reason that you'd apply labels to a package that you are sending. Several headers may be applied to each packet.

A host sending data to another host is like me sending a package to somebody—for instance, sending a bicycle to my sister in another state. The bicycle represents data that is going to be transferred to another host. To send the bicycle, I have to follow certain rules, or protocols. I put the bicycle into a package, or maybe more than one package if it doesn't fit into a single package. In this example, the packages represent packets.

Even after the bicycle is inside the packages, it is not going anywhere until I put some addressing information on it. There are protocols for putting addresses on the packages: I must use my sister's correct name as well as her correct address. The address label must include the pieces of information necessary to get the packages to the correct destination—for example, her street address, city, state, and zip code. This is similar to TCP/IP putting addressing information headers on the packets that are being transmitted. I also put my return address on the labels, which is similar to a data packet including its source information. There is a proper place for all this addressing information, and I must correctly fill it in on every package or the packages will not get there. Finally, I indicate the order in which to open the packages by writing "1 of 6, 2 of 6, etc." on them. This will let my sister know which package to open first, second, and so on, so that she can easily reassemble the bike.

After the packages are ready to go, I need to decide which delivery service to use. The packages' format depends on the delivery service I choose: If I use Federal Express, I will put the packages into FedEx boxes; if I use United Parcel Service, I will put the packages into a UPS format. Similarly, packets are encapsulated into a format that is appropriate for the physical network that the sending host is located on. If the host is on an Ethernet network, the packet must be in the appropriate format to travel on an Ethernet network. If it's on a Token Ring network, it must be in the Token Ring format. **Encapsulation** is a fancy word for wrapping up the packet into the appropriate package or format.

headers
Bits of information attached to each packet that usually include addressing and routing details; the information acts like a little sticky note on the packet.

encapsulation
The wrapping of a packet into the appropriate package or format.

Because I'm on a UPS route, I call Mike, the UPS man, and ask him to pick up the packages. Neither Mike nor I deliver the packages. Instead, the data, packaged in the appropriate format, moves through the transport system, being transferred from one location to the next. The packages might take different routes, but they will get to the same destination. They are delivered to the destination based on the address that I put on the labels. If there is a problem with the delivery, the system will let me know because I put my return address on the packages.

After the packages arrive, my sister opens them. She can reassemble the bicycle based on the information that was on the labels. Similarly, the recipient of the data packet can assemble the data based on the information in the packets' headers.

My sister discards the packing material after she uses the pertinent information from the labels. All she really wants is the bicycle; the packaging was used only to send the bicycle to the correct destination and in the correct order. When using TCP/IP to transport data, a packet is built with several headers, which are discarded after the important information has been used and the data has been delivered to the requesting application.

The illustration below shows Harry the Host sending data to Sally the Host. Notice that the data has been fragmented into several packets and that each packet includes sequence numbers. At the receiving host, Sally reassembles the data back to its unfragmented format.

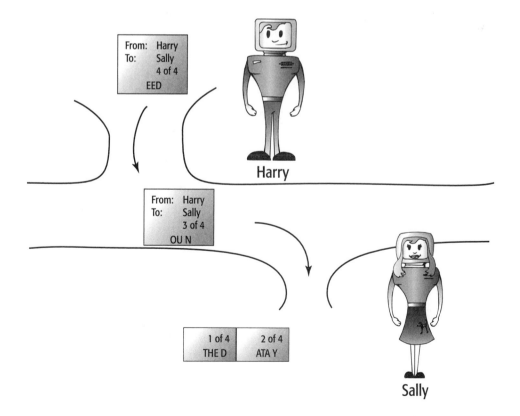

Why We Need Protocols and Standards

Rules—or protocols and standards—are important to ensure compatibility between different kinds of things. As more and more hardware and software vendors began joining the technology explosion, there was no guarantee that any of their products would be able to work with one another. A system had to be put in place so that hardware and software consumers would not get burned by buying incompatible systems.

For example, let's say that I own a small business and I want to buy some new computer equipment. I go out and find some hardware and software that will make my business run smoother and more effectively. All the vendors tell me how great their hardware and software is, so I buy it. I've been sold the dream of how my new automated office will function and how I'll have nothing but spare time. I've been told that everything works together and that my small business will be successful as a result.

However, I bought some hardware from one vendor, some software from another, some other hardware from another vendor, and more software from yet another. And guess what? None of the stuff works together. I just spent a ton of money, and now I'm spending all my time calling for support. All the nice support people are telling me it's the other vendor's software or hardware that is causing the problem.

To keep this scenario from happening, standards and protocols were developed. If the hardware and software vendors were all working with the same guidelines—the same standards and protocols—then their hardware and software should all work together. The hardware vendor would continue to make money selling his hardware, the software vendor would continue to make money selling his software, and I would make money in my small- to medium-sized automated business. I would be happy to buy more hardware and software because it works and it serves my purposes.

Developing protocols is an ongoing, ever changing science. New protocols are constantly under development and testing, and they are improved as the need arises. As the industry is increasing so dynamically and rapidly, more protocols are unleashed to handle the boom. However, before a protocol is accepted and widely implemented, it has to pass rigorous testing. A standard framework is used to help design, compare, test, and evaluate protocols.

The OSI Reference Model

For network communications to take place, hundreds of questions must be answered by a set of protocols. Evaluating and working with these hundreds of questions would be unmanageable. So, in 1977 the **International Standards Organization (ISO)** adopted the **Open Standards Interconnection (OSI)** model. The OSI model breaks down the many tasks involved in moving data from one host to another. Now instead of having hundreds of questions to answer, the OSI model gives us a reference to work with. The hundreds of questions are divided into seven smaller, more manageable groups of questions. The seven groups are called **layers**.

The OSI reference model is exactly that; it is only a model. If we continue to think of the model as a set of questions that have to be answered, then the protocols are the answers. Any one protocol may answer only a few of the questions, or in other words, address specific layers in the model. By combining multiple protocols into a protocol suite, we can answer all the questions posed by the model.

The OSI model was created by making a list of most computer networking topics, such as routing, reliability, and sequencing. From this list, all the topics were categorized by how they are used in network communications. Within each layer, several topics are discussed. Breaking down this huge task of data communication into seven layers makes the task more manageable.

NOTE

The seven layers of the OSI model are explained in the following sections.

The OSI reference model functions as a baseline for comparison to any protocol suite. As such you can use the OSI model—or the DoD model, which you'll learn about later in this chapter—to help understand how the parts of TCP/IP work.

This baseline function of the OSI model is similar to a model home. When designing your new home, a model can be used as a baseline. Everyone in the neighborhood also uses the model home as reference to help make the choices in the new homes that they are building. All the homes will vary slightly from the model, but the model provides a means for comparison. In the same way, you can compare any protocol suite to the OSI reference model because protocols are designed from this model. The OSI model acts as a baseline for creating and comparing networking protocols.

International Standards Organization (ISO)
The organization that ratified the OSI model.

Open Standards Interconnection model (OSI)
A seven-layer model used to break down the many tasks involved in moving data from one host to another.

layers
A portion of the OSI model that is used to categorize specific concerns.

The Seven Layers of the OSI Model

The goal of the OSI model is to break down the task of data communication into simple steps. These steps are called layers, and the OSI model is made up of seven distinct layers. Each layer has certain responsibilities.

The seven layers of the OSI model are:

- ◇ Application
- ◇ Presentation
- ◇ Session
- ◇ Transport
- ◇ Network
- ◇ Data-Link
- ◇ Physical

You will learn about the responsibilities of each of these layers in the following sections. The following illustration shows the seven-layered OSI model.

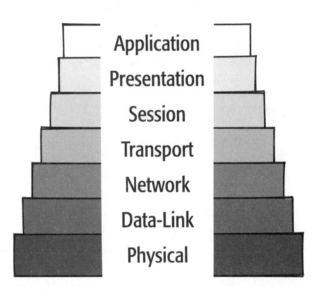

Responsibilities of Each Layer

The purpose of each layer in the OSI model is to provide services to the layer above it while shielding the upper level from what happens below. The higher layers do not need to know how the data got there or what happened at the lower layers.

The following illustration shows how data moves through the seven layers of the OSI model. Here, Harry the Host is transmitting data onto a network. He could be saving a file from his word processing application to a file server, for example. As the data moves down the seven layers toward the network, each layer puts a little bit of information called a header on the packet. The exact contents of each header depend on the protocols enabled at each layer of the protocol suite.

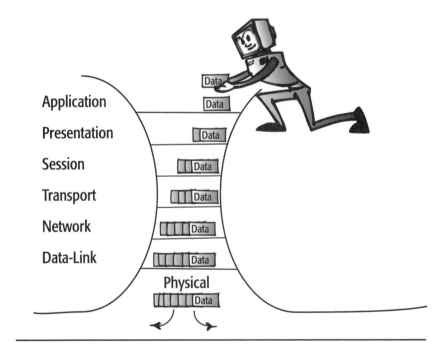

The Application Layer

The top layer of the OSI model is the Application layer. The purpose of the Application layer is to manage communications between applications. A standard Application layer program such as FTP or SMTP interacts with a program that is running at the local workstation. The programmer who has written a word processing application writes the program to interact with a standard application that exists at the Application layer. The word processor uses the standard network application to save, copy, or delete files.

The Presentation Layer

The Presentation layer is the layer below the Application layer and above the Session layer. The Presentation layer adds structure to packets of data being exchanged. The primary job of the Presentation layer is to ensure that the message gets transmitted in a language or syntax that the receiving computer can understand. The protocols at the Presentation layer may translate the data into an understandable syntax and then compress and maybe encrypt the data before passing it down to the Session layer.

The Session Layer

The Session layer is below the Presentation layer. It controls the dialog during communications. The Session layer protocols set up sessions, or connections. These protocols cover such topics as how to establish a connection, how to use a connection, and how to break down the connection when a session is completed. After a connection is established, the Session layer protocols check for transmission errors. The Session layer also adds control headers to the data packets during the exchange of data.

The Transport Layer

Below the Session layer is the Transport layer. The Transport layer can guarantee that packets are received. The Transport layer also can establish a connection and send acknowledgments as packets are received. The protocols in this layer provide the means to establish, maintain, and release connections for the hosts involved in communication.

The Network Layer

The Network layer, which is below the Transport layer, is responsible for routing the packet based on its logical address. The Network layer fragments and reassembles packets if necessary. It also moves the packets of data from the source to the destination and across networks if necessary.

The Data-Link Layer

Below the Network layer is the Data-Link layer, which is where the data is prepared for final delivery to the network. The packet is encapsulated into a frame (which is a term used to describe the bundle of binary data). Protocols at this layer aid in the addressing and error detection of data being transferred.

The Data-Link layer is made up of two sublayers: the Logical Link Control (LLC) sublayer and the Media Access Control (MAC) sublayer. Each sublayer provides its own services. The LLC sublayer is the interface between Network layer protocols and the media access method, for example, Ethernet or Token Ring. The MAC sublayer handles the connection to the physical media, such as twisted-pair or coaxial cabling.

The Physical Layer

At the bottom of the OSI model is the Physical layer. The topics at this layer determine how the sending and receiving bits of data move along the network's wire. Think of the actual bits moving from the network card on your computer to the wire on the network. At this layer we talk about the data in bits and packets.

Mnemonics to Help You Remember the Seven Layers

Remembering the order of the OSI model's seven layers will be helpful in any discussion of any protocol or protocol suite. Some mnemonics that might help you remember the seven layers are:

From top to bottom:

All People Seem To Need Data Processing

Aunt Paula Says To Never Drink Poison

From bottom to top:

Please Do Not Throw Sausage Pizza Away

Please Do Not Take Sales Persons' Advice

Paul Dumped Nancy To See Paula Abdul

How the OSI Model Is Used

Packet creation starts at the top of the OSI model. The Application layer gets the data to be transmitted and passes the packet down to the Presentation layer, where another header is put on the packet. The Presentation layer passes the packet down, and each layer puts a header on the packet until the Physical layer gets the packet. The Physical layer merges the packet onto the network wire, and the data continues on its way to the destination.

At the destination, the packet moves in the opposite direction, from the bottom of the model to the top. The Physical layer at the destination protocol stack takes the packet off of the wire and passes it up to the Data-Link layer. The Data-Link layer examines the header that the sending Data-Link layer put on the packet. If this is not the destination for this packet, the packet is discarded. If this is the destination for this packet, the Data-Link layer protocols strip off the Data-Link header that the sender had put onto the packet and pass the rest of the packet up to the Network layer. This continues at every layer until the data reaches the top of the stack.

In this way, each layer of the sending host communicates with the same layer of the receiving host. This is called **peer-layer communication**.

The illustration below depicts peer-layer communication. Each layer in the sending host communicates with its peer layer in the receiving host. Notice that each layer has specific responsibilities that aid in communicating with the other host.

TCP/IP and the DoD Model

The TCP/IP protocol suite was developed before the OSI model was published. As a result, it does not use the OSI model as a reference. TCP/IP was developed using the **Department of Defense (DoD)** reference model. It's important to be familiar with the OSI model, though, because OSI is used to compare the TCP/IP suite with other protocol suites.

Unlike the OSI model, the DoD reference model has four layers. Still, the DoD model answers the same questions about network communications as the OSI model. In the following chapters, you will learn about each of the layers in the DoD model.

The four layers of the DoD model are

Application   Covers the topics of Application, Presentation, and Session in the OSI model. The Application layer is covered in detail in Chapter 5.

Transport   Covers the topics of Transport from the OSI model. The Transport layer is covered in detail in Chapter 4.

Internet   Covers the topics of Network from the OSI model. The Internet layer is examined in detail in Chapter 3.

Network Interface Layer   Covers the topics of Data-Link and Physical from the OSI model. The Network Interface layer is examined in detail in Chapter 3.

The following table compares the OSI and DoD models. Notice how some of the layers in the DoD model encompass several layers of the OSI model.

OSI Model	DoD or TCP/IP Model
Application layer	Application layer
Presentation layer	
Session layer	
Transport layer	Transport layer
Network layer	Internet layer
Data-Link layer	Network Interface layer
Physical layer	

Department of Defense (DoD)
The branch of the United States military maintaining national defense.

Review Questions

1. What is a protocol?

_____

2. What is a packet?

_____

3. Why was the OSI model created?

_____

4. List the seven layers of the OSI model.

_____

_____

_____

_____

_____

_____

5. List the four layers of the DoD model.

_____

_____

_____

_____

6. List three protocol suites.

_____

_____

_____

7. Data is moved across the network in manageable chunks of data called:

_____

8. Labels on a package are analogous to _____ on a packet.

9. Which layer of the OSI model has been divided into two sublayers?

_____

10. What are the two sublayers of the Data-Link layer?

_____

_____

Chapter

3

The Network Interface and Internet Layers

The Network Interface layer and the Internet layer address and route packets. These layers interact with the network by defining how the packets are moved to and from the network. Protocols place headers onto the packet like labels being placed on a package that is being mailed. As each packet is received at a host, it is examined to see if it needs to be processed or discarded.

In this chapter you will learn about:

 The Network Interface layer

 Hardware addresses

 Broadcast addresses

 The Internet layer

 Internet Protocol (IP)

 Address Resolution Protocol (ARP)

 Internet Control Message Protocol (ICMP)

 Internet Group Message Protocol (IGMP)

The Network Interface Layer

The lowest layer in the TCP/IP stack is the **Network Interface layer**. The primary responsibility of the Network Interface layer is to define how a computer connects to a network. This is an important part of the data delivery process because data must be delivered to a particular host through a connection to a network, and data leaving a host has to follow the rules of the network that it is on.

The TCP/IP Network Interface layer does not regulate the type of network that the host is on, but the network that the host is on dictates the driver that the Network Interface layer uses. The host can be on an Ethernet, Token Ring, or Fiber Distributed Data Interface (FDDI), for instance, or on any other **network topology**. The host has to follow the rules for transmitting and receiving data according to the topology of the network.

One way to understand how the host interacts with the Network Interface layer is to compare it to a similar real-life example. For instance, say you are going to send a get-well-soon card and a chocolate cake to your grandmother in the hospital. You are in charge of packaging and addressing the cake and card, but then you turn it over to another system for delivery. You might use one of the private companies offering overnight services or you might use the United States Postal Service; that is not the critical component of this transaction. You must follow the rules established by the service you are using, such as how to address the package, how much to pay for postage, and how to include your return address. When Grandma receives the package, it doesn't really matter how it got there, she is just pleased that it did. How the Network Interface layer at a host interacts with the network that it is connected to is analogous to how you would interact with the postal service.

Network Interface layer
Lowest layer of the DoD model, it acts as a host's connection, or interface, to the network.

network topology
Describes how a network is connected and how each host knows when and how to transmit and receive data.

NOTE

The Network Interface layer is sometimes referred to as the Data-Link layer.

The Network Interface layer is like the receiving department of the hospital. Employees there receive many packages and must decide which to pass up to patients. After they see that your package is addressed correctly, they pass it up to your grandmother. She processes the package by opening it to eat the cake and read the card that you sent.

Similarly, the Network Interface layer is used to receive packets and to send packets. As a packet is received by a network card, the Network Interface layer acts like the receiving department at the hospital and determines whether to pass the packet up the protocol stack for processing based on the hardware address. As a packet is being created, it eventually gets passed down to the Network Interface layer to be put onto the network.

At the Network Interface layer, a header is applied that contains addressing information. Contained within the header is an address called a hardware address, which you will learn about in the next section. The following graphic shows several hosts on a network. Each host has a mailbox through which it sends packets out onto the network and receives packets from the network.

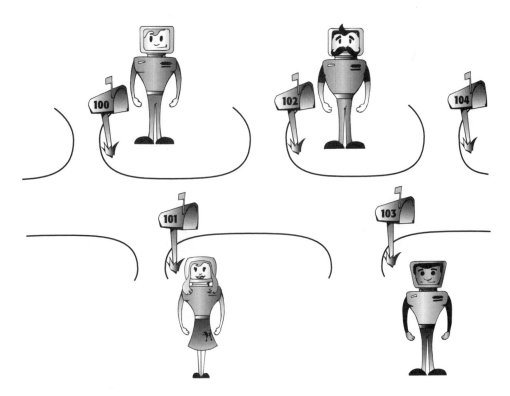

Hardware Address

Within every packet of data is a header that contains addressing information. This header enables the packet to arrive at the correct location. This addressing information comes from a physical address that is burned into every **network interface card** when the card is manufactured. This address will not change for the life of the card. This burned-in address can be called any of the following:

- ◇ Hardware address
- ◇ Media Access Control (MAC) address
- ◇ Ethernet address
- ◇ Physical address
- ◇ Network Interface Card (NIC) address

The hardware address is unique to all the network cards ever manufactured. It is a 12-character hexadecimal address. A hardware address looks similar to this:

00:A0:C9:0F:92:A5

NOTE

The three most common numbering systems used in the computer industry are **binary**, **decimal**, and **hexadecimal**. The hexadecimal numbering system uses the same 0 to 9 digits as decimal, then uses A, B, C, D, E, and F to represent 10, 11, 12, 13, 14, and 15. The decimal 16 is represented in hexadecimal as 10.

The first six of these hexadecimal characters represent the manufacturer and are unique to the network card's manufacturer. The last six characters form a unique serial number that the card's manufacturer has assigned to it.

Therefore, if a network card manufacturer doesn't use the same serial number twice, and no two manufacturers use the same manufacturer ID, no two network cards will ever have the same hardware address. In the same way that a Social Security number uniquely identifies a person, a hardware address uniquely identifies a network card.

---

network interface card

A piece of hardware that is used to connect a host to a network; every host must have one in order to connect to a network.

---

binary

The base-2 numbering system that computers use to represent data; it consists of only two numbers, 0 and 1.

---

decimal

A numbering system that uses 0, 1, 2, 3, 4, 5, 6, 7, 8, 9.

---

hexadecimal

A base-16 numbering system containing 16 sequential numbers (including 0) as base units before adding a new position for the next number; the hexadecimal system uses the numbers 0–9 and then the letters A–F.

TIP

For all TCP/IP communication to occur, the sender/builder of the packet must know the destination hardware address.

broadcast packet
A packet that is addressed to all hosts; the broadcast address is a universal address enabling all hosts to receive the packet.

For a TCP/IP packet to be delivered, it must contain the destination's hardware address. As each packet arrives at the network interface card, the portion of the packet that contains the target hardware address is examined to see whether the packet is intended for that host. If the target hardware address matches that of the receiving network interface card, or if the packet was broadcast, the packet is passed up the stack for processing. If the packet's target hardware address is different, then the packet is discarded.

This process is similar to going to the mailbox to check the mail. You may look through the mail while you are still standing at the mailbox. As you are looking at the pieces, you check to see to whom each letter is addressed. If it is addressed to you, you begin to process it; if it is not to you, you ignore it. If an envelope is addressed to "resident," you also start to process it and see whether it applies to you. The address of "resident" is like a broadcast address in a packet: The broadcast mail is sent out hoping to find someone that it applies to.

Broadcast Packets

Every packet must be addressed to a host. As the packets move through the network, every host will examine every packet to see if each is addressed to that host's unique hardware address.

A packet may be intended for all hosts on a network. This type of packet is called a **broadcast packet**. A broadcast packet contains the target hardware address of FF:FF:FF:FF:FF:FF.

The Internet Layer

The **Internet layer** of the TCP/IP model lies between the Network Interface layer and the Transport layer. (The Transport layer is discussed in Chapter 4.) The Internet layer contains the protocols that are responsible for addressing and **routing** of packets. The Internet layer contains several protocols, including:

◆ Internet Protocol (IP)

◆ Address Resolution Protocol (ARP)

◆ Internet Control Message Protocol (ICMP)

◆ Internet Group Message Protocol (IGMP)

In the following sections, you will learn about each of these protocols.

In the preceding section, you learned that for TCP/IP communication to be successful, the packet examined by the Network Interface layer must have a hardware address in its header. As the packet moves up to the Internet layer, it also needs to contain an **IP address**. Using the IP address, the Internet layer provides the necessary protocols to determine the hardware address for routing the packet to the destination.

NOTE

IP addressing is covered in detail in Chapter 6.

The illustration below shows the protocols at the Internet layer. Each of these protocols is discussed in the following sections.

Internet layer
Layer between the Network Interface and Transport layers of the DoD model; protocols at the Internet layer focus on addressing.

routing
The process of determining which is the next path to send a packet so that it gets to its destination.

IP address
An address that IP uses to identify a unique network and host.

Internet Protocol (IP)

The Internet Protocol is the primary protocol at the Internet layer of the TCP/IP stack. This protocol is responsible for determining the source and destination IP addresses of every packet.

The network administrator assigns every host on a network a unique IP address. Whereas the hardware address refers to the physical network card, the IP address refers to a **logical address** that the network administrator has assigned to the host. Every host on a TCP/IP network has a unique IP address. An example of an IP address is:

    192.168.2.51

This logical address is assigned by the administrator to the host and must be unique on its network. A portion of the IP address describes the TCP/IP network that the host is on, and a portion describes the unique host address on that network.

The street address where you live is like a logical address. A letter that is addressed to you will be delivered to your house because of this logical address. If you move to another house, your address will change, and letters to you will have to be sent to this new address—but the one who the letter is being delivered to, you, is still the same.

As a packet is being passed down the TCP/IP stack, a source and target IP address are put into an IP header. IP determines whether the destination is local or remote as compared to the source host. The target is local if IP determines that the target is on the same network, and it is remote if the target is on another network. IP can make this determination based on the IP address of the target and the **subnet mask** of the source host.

The subnet mask is a required parameter of every TCP/IP address that is used to separate the network and host portions of that address.

logical address
This address can be modified; it refers only to the host.

subnet mask
A parameter included with every IP address that highlights the network portion of the IP address.

NOTE

Subnet masks are covered in Chapter 7.

Determining Whether the Destination is Local or Remote

IP needs to determine how to get a packet to the destination. If the destination is addressed to a host on the local network, TCP/IP can communicate directly with the destination host. If the host is on a **remote network**, TCP/IP needs to send the packet through the **default gateway**.

A default gateway, also called a **router**, is the address of a host on the network that offers a route off of the network. In other words, the default gateway is the door providing access off of the network.

TCP/IP's communication process is similar to mailing a package. If you want to send a package to someone who lives on the same street that you do, you'd be able to deliver it yourself. If you mail a package to someone who lives on any other street, the package would go to the post office, and then the post office could figure out how to get the package to its destination. The post office is like a default gateway.

In the illustration below, the router is like a post office that routes the packets to the correct network.

remote network

A network other than the one that the host is on; a remote network is on the other side of a router.

default gateway

A parameter included with the router's IP address that packets are sent to en route to a remote network.

router

A host that interfaces with other networks and can move packets from one network to another.

The next illustration shows Harry the Host sending a packet to Sally the Host. The IP protocol in Harry's TCP/IP stack will examine the destination address (Sally's) and determine that Sally is local to Harry. The destination host is local when IP determines that both the sending and destination hosts have the same network portion in their IP addresses.

routing table
A table that contains the addresses indicating the best routes to other networks.

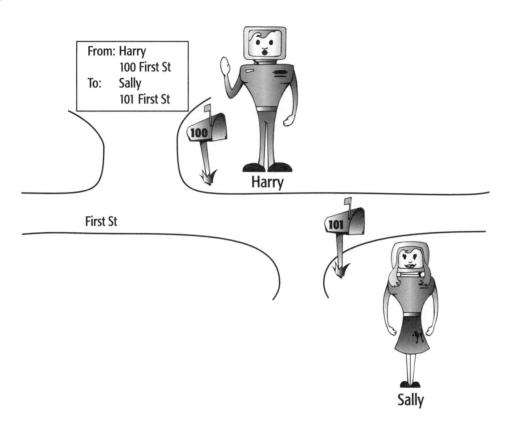

```
From: Harry
       100 First St
To:    Sally
       101 First St
```

100

Harry

First St

101

Sally

If the target host is local, IP needs to get the hardware address for the target. If the target host is remote, IP looks in its **routing table** for an explicit route to that network. If there is an explicit route, IP needs to get the hardware address of the gateway listed in the routing table. If there is no explicit route, IP needs to get the hardware address for the default gateway.

Determining the Hardware Address

The following flowchart outlines the decision process that TCP/IP uses to decide whose hardware address is required to send a packet.

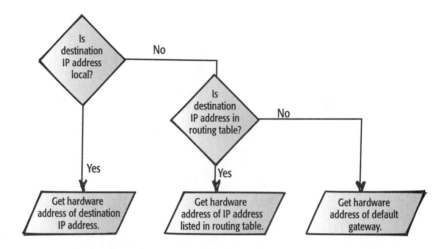

When assigning the IP address of the host, a network administrator will type in the address of the default gateway as one of the TCP/IP parameters. (The packet will be sent to the default gateway's hardware address if the packet is destined for another network.) The default gateway then determines whether the target IP address is on one of its other interfaces or whether the default gateway needs to forward the packet to another router.

Using another analogy, this is similar to going to an airport and trying to get to a destination. If there is a direct route from the airport to your destination, you are sent to your destination. If no direct route exists, you are sent on a route that will get you closer to your destination. If the target is on one of the other interfaces, IP can send the packet through that interface onto the destination network. IP on the gateway strips off the original IP header and puts a new IP header on the packet. The gateway is now the source, and the destination of the packet is either the actual target or the next gateway on its way to the target network.

In the next step, IP uses the **Address Resolution Protocol (ARP)** to get the hardware address of the destination host. ARP is like a detective who will find the hardware address of the destination host based on the IP address that the Internet Protocol is asking for.

Address Resolution Protocol (ARP)

ARP is a protocol that can **resolve** an IP address to a hardware address. After the hardware address is resolved, ARP maintains that information for a short time. Because the host wants to communicate with another host, but only has the IP address, ARP will ask, "Hey, what is your hardware address?" and wait for an answer.

The first place that ARP looks to resolve an IP address to a hardware address is in **ARP cache**. ARP cache is an area in random access memory (RAM) where ARP keeps the IP and hardware addresses that have been resolved. If ARP can find the IP and hardware addresses in ARP cache, the packet is addressed to the hardware address with no further resolution. If the IP address is not in ARP cache, ARP will initiate an **ARP request** broadcast.

After an IP address is resolved to a hardware address, it is stored in ARP cache for two minutes. If IP requests resolution again to the same IP address within those two minutes, the entry will stay in ARP cache another two minutes. An entry can stay in ARP cache for a maximum of ten minutes; then it will be removed from cache regardless of whether it has been referenced within the last two minutes.

The screen capture below shows the ARP cache. The cache contains three types of entries: the IP address in the first column, the hardware address in the second column, and an indication of how the entry got into ARP cache in the third column. An entry in ARP cache is dynamic when an address has been discovered through broadcast, and static when the address has been manually added.

```
C:\>ARP -A

Interface: 209.132.94.125 on Interface 2
  Internet Address      Physical Address      Type
  209.132.94.113        00-a0-24-35-d1-df     dynamic
  209.132.94.114        00-a0-24-87-f0-f0     dynamic
  209.132.94.115        00-a0-24-87-ec-e2     dynamic
  209.132.94.119        00-a0-24-87-f3-c0     dynamic
  209.132.94.120        00-a0-24-87-f3-b3     dynamic
  209.132.94.121        00-a0-24-87-f3-bf     dynamic

C:\>_
```

resolve
To translate a logical to a physical address.

ARP cache
An area in RAM that holds recently resolved IP-to-hardware address resolutions.

ARP request
A broadcast packet that seeks to resolve an IP address to a hardware address.

Using Broadcast to Resolve a Hardware Address

If ARP does not find the IP address in ARP cache, the ARP protocol initiates an ARP request. This request is broadcast on the local network. In the following illustration, Harry's ARP is trying to get resolution for the IP address of 209.132.94.101. ARP broadcasts a packet onto the network that basically says:

"HEY, WHOEVER IS 209.132.94.101, I NEED YOUR HARDWARE ADDRESS!"

The ARP broadcast is addressed to every host by setting the destination hardware address to FF:FF:FF:FF:FF:FF. The ARP broadcast contains the IP address of the requested destination so that the intended recipient is identified. The ARP broadcast also contains the source's hardware address. Including the source's hardware address expedites the reply from the destination host. After the destination receives and recognizes that the ARP broadcast is intended for it, the destination puts the source IP address and hardware address into its own ARP cache. Because the source's hardware address is in ARP cache, the address will already be known when the ARP reply is sent back to the original source.

The Network Interface and Internet Layers

As the ARP packet is received at each host, the network interface card takes the packet off of the wire and passes it up through the Network Interface layer to the Internet layer and ARP. ARP at the destination examines the packet to see whether the packet is asking for that host's hardware address. If the ARP request is not for that host, the packet is discarded. If it does have that host's hardware address, the IP and hardware address of the source is put into ARP cache and an ARP reply to the source is created. The target's hardware address is included in the **ARP reply**. When the ARP reply is received, the IP and hardware addresses are placed into ARP cache for two minutes.

In the illustration below, Sally the host responds to the ARP request with a packet that contains her IP address and hardware address. This ARP reply is sent directly to Harry because the ARP request had his IP and hardware addresses.

ARP reply
A packet that is returned to the sender of the ARP request and that includes the IP address and hardware address that was requested.

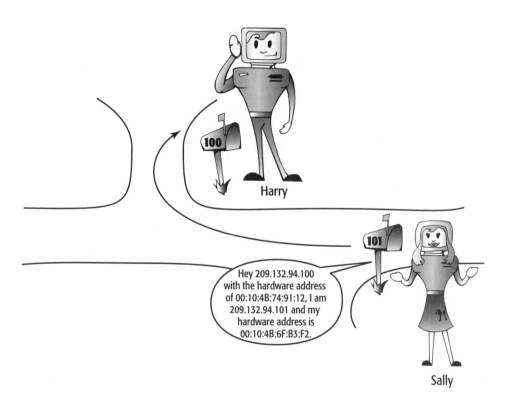

ARP Packets

The following screen shot shows two ARP packets that were captured from a network. The first packet says that it is an ARP request and the target IP is 209.132.94.101.

The bottom portion of the graphic shows the contents of the first packet. You can see that the ARP request packet was broadcast to all hosts (destination FFFFFFFFFFFF) in the ETHERNET section. This ARP request came from a source host whose hardware address is 00104B749112. In the ARP section of this packet, the sender's hardware and protocol addresses and the target's protocol address are filled in, but not the target's hardware address. The purpose of this packet is to request that the host with the protocol address of 209.132.94.101 reply and fill in the hardware address section.

```
Frame Src MAC Addr  Dst MAC Addr  Protocol Description                                                              S
1     HARRY         *BROADCAST    ARP_RARP ARP: Request, Target IP: 209.132.94.101
2     SALLY         HARRY         ARP_RARP ARP: Reply, Target IP: 209.132.94.100 Target Hdwr Addr: 00104B749112

FRAME: Base frame properties
ETHERNET: ETYPE = 0x0806 : Protocol = ARP:  Address Resolution Protocol
  ETHERNET: Destination address : FFFFFFFFFFFF
  ETHERNET: Source address : 00104B749112
  ETHERNET: Frame Length : 60 (0x003C)
  ETHERNET: Ethernet Type : 0x0806 (ARP:  Address Resolution Protocol)
  ETHERNET: Ethernet Data: Number of data bytes remaining = 46 (0x002E)
ARP_RARP: ARP: Request, Target IP: 209.132.94.101
  ARP_RARP: Hardware Address Space = 1 (0x1)
  ARP_RARP: Protocol Address Space = 2048 (0x800)
  ARP_RARP: Hardware Address Length = 6 (0x6)
  ARP_RARP: Protocol Address Length = 4 (0x4)
  ARP_RARP: Opcode = 1 (0x1)
  ARP_RARP: Sender's Hardware Address = 00104B749112
  ARP_RARP: Sender's Protocol Address = 209.132.94.100
  ARP_RARP: Target's Hardware Address = 000000000000
  ARP_RARP: Target's Protocol Address = 209.132.94.101
  ARP_RARP: Frame Padding
```

The following screen shot shows the contents of the ARP reply. The reply is a new packet and is sent from the target host. The target host is now the sender because it is sending back the requested information. In this reply packet, the source lets the destination know the source's hardware address.

```
Frame Src MAC Addr  Dst MAC Addr  Protocol Description                                                              S
1     HARRY         *BROADCAST    ARP_RARP ARP: Request, Target IP: 209.132.94.101
2     SALLY         HARRY         ARP_RARP ARP: Reply, Target IP: 209.132.94.100 Target Hdwr Addr: 00104B749112

FRAME: Base frame properties
ETHERNET: ETYPE = 0x0806 : Protocol = ARP:  Address Resolution Protocol
  ETHERNET: Destination address : 00104B749112
  ETHERNET: Source address : 00104B6FB3F2
  ETHERNET: Frame Length : 60 (0x003C)
  ETHERNET: Ethernet Type : 0x0806 (ARP:  Address Resolution Protocol)
  ETHERNET: Ethernet Data: Number of data bytes remaining = 46 (0x002E)
ARP_RARP: ARP: Reply, Target IP: 209.132.94.100 Target Hdwr Addr: 00104B749112
  ARP_RARP: Hardware Address Space = 1 (0x1)
  ARP_RARP: Protocol Address Space = 2048 (0x800)
  ARP_RARP: Hardware Address Length = 6 (0x6)
  ARP_RARP: Protocol Address Length = 4 (0x4)
  ARP_RARP: Opcode = 2 (0x2)
  ARP_RARP: Sender's Hardware Address = 00104B6FB3F2
  ARP_RARP: Sender's Protocol Address = 209.132.94.101
  ARP_RARP: Target's Hardware Address = 00104B749112
  ARP_RARP: Target's Protocol Address = 209.132.94.100
  ARP_RARP: Frame Padding
```

Internet Control Message Protocol (ICMP)

ICMP is a protocol used primarily for sending error messages, performing diagnostics, and controlling the flow of data. An example of an error message and of flow control is an ICMP **source-quench** packet sent by a router to a source host to tell the host to slow down because the router is overloaded.

Routers let hosts send data as fast as possible—unless traffic at the router is getting too heavy. Then, a router will send the host a source-quench message as an ICMP packet, requesting that the host slow down. After the host receives a source-quench message, the host will slow down and then slowly increase the speed again until another source-quench message is sent.

The router's action is similar to a real-life situation you might be familiar with. When driving in the car with the kids in the back, I will let them play and get louder until finally I will send back a source-quench message. The message says, "You'd better quiet down; you're getting too loud!" The kids will immediately quiet down. Then they will slowly start ramping up again until I have to send back another source-quench message. The kids will make as much noise as they can get away with in the same way that the hosts will constantly be trying to send data as fast as the router can handle it.

Performing Diagnostics with ICMP and Ping

As stated earlier, the ICMP protocol is used for performing diagnostics. An example of using ICMP as a diagnostic tool is with the **Ping** utility. Ping stands for Packet InterNet Groper.

An administrator uses the Ping utility to send four ICMP echo request packets to the destination host and to ask that the destination host reply to these packets. ICMP places a small amount of data and requests that the data get sent back. If the data returns, the administrator can assume successful connectivity to the destination. If the ICMP packet does not return, then a connectivity problem exists.

To ping another host from a command prompt, type:

```
Ping ip address
```

source-quench
An ICMP packet that is sent to slow down the transmission at the source.

Ping
Packet InterNet Groper; a software utility that tests connectivity between two TCP/IP hosts.

Examining Ping Packets

In the screen shot below, the source host (209.132.94.100) pinged the destination host (209.132.94.101).

Frame	Src MAC Addr	Dst MAC Addr	Protocol	Description
33	HARRY	*BROADCAST	ARP_RARP	ARP: Request, Target IP: 209.132.94.101
34	SALLY	HARRY	ARP_RARP	ARP: Reply, Target IP: 209.132.94.100 Target Hdwr Addr: 00104B749112
35	HARRY	SALLY	ICMP	Echo, From 209.132.94.100 To 209.132.94.101
36	SALLY	HARRY	ICMP	Echo Reply, To 209.132.94.100 From 209.132.94.101
37	HARRY	SALLY	ICMP	Echo, From 209.132.94.100 To 209.132.94.101
38	SALLY	HARRY	ICMP	Echo Reply, To 209.132.94.100 From 209.132.94.101
39	HARRY	SALLY	ICMP	Echo, From 209.132.94.100 To 209.132.94.101
40	SALLY	HARRY	ICMP	Echo Reply, To 209.132.94.100 From 209.132.94.101
41	HARRY	SALLY	ICMP	Echo, From 209.132.94.100 To 209.132.94.101
42	SALLY	HARRY	ICMP	Echo Reply, To 209.132.94.100 From 209.132.94.101

The screen shot shows:

1. (Frame 1) An ARP request is broadcast for the target 209.132.94.101.
2. (Frame 2) An ARP reply is sent to the source at 209.132.94.100 with the target's hardware address.
3. (Frame 3) An ICMP packet is sent from the source 209.132.94.100 to the destination 209.132.94.101 requesting an "echo."
4. (Frame 4) An ICMP echo reply is sent from the destination 209.132.94.101 to the source 209.132.94.100.
5. (Frames 5–10) Steps 3 and 4 are repeated three more times.

Looking at captured packets is like eavesdropping on the hosts' conversation. Sending a little ICMP packet to another host is an excellent method of testing connectivity. It takes virtually no overhead for the destination to respond with an ICMP reply.

Although almost no overhead is required, some sites, such as www.microsoft.com, will not respond to ICMP request packets. The enormous amount of ping-request traffic Microsoft was receiving caused the overhead to get excessive, and so their servers no longer reply to such requests. A network administrator has set up a filter as well so that ICMP echo packets are filtered or dropped at the **firewall** for security purposes. A company may not want outsiders pinging or "groping" inside their network.

Internet Group Management Protocol (IGMP)

IGMP is a protocol that enables one host to send one **stream** of data to many hosts at the same time. Most TCP/IP connections consist of one host sending data to one other host, or possibly to all hosts via a broadcast. In contrast, IGMP packets are directed to a **reserved IP address**, and any hosts that would like to receive the data stream have to listen at the address. In other words, the host does not wait to receive data at its own address—it has to actively request the data that is sent to the reserved IP address.

The destination IP address used by IGMP is called a **multicast address.** These reserved IP addresses cannot be assigned to a host. With special software, a TCP/IP host can "listen" for data that is being sent to a multicast address. When several hosts are listening for data at a specific address and data is sent to that address, all the hosts receive the data. All these packets contain an IGMP header.

stream
A series of packets sent without waiting for acknowledgments.

reserved IP address
An IP address that cannot be used as a valid host address.

multicast address
A reserved IP address that IGMP uses for streaming data.

NOTE

Multicast addresses are covered in detail in Chapter 6.

Many devices on a network use IGMP packets to exchange data. Some routing protocols use IGMP to exchange routing tables. Windows Internet Naming Service (WINS) can use IGMP to exchange databases. Across the Internet, many sites are using IGMP packets to move streams of data to many hosts concurrently.

The concept of multicast is similar to a garden hose that has a bunch of small pinholes in it. As a stream of water gushes down the hose, the water is received by many. The water represents the one stream of data and the pinholes represent the hosts that receive it. In this way, the stream is sent only once, but many can receive it.

Sending Streaming Audio and Video with IGMP

IGMP can be used as the protocol for sending streaming audio or streaming video when the data needs to go from one source to many receivers. Rather than address and track each packet to every host, which would be impossible, the data is streamed to a multicast address, and the recipients listen and receive at that address.

Again, multicasting is like a garden hose with several small holes in it: The water is not directed to any one place, but it is dispersed to many. The following illustration shows a server sending some IGMP audio packets. The host "sings" the broadcast. Some of the other hosts listen and some don't. Whether Harry gets the data is not important to the sender.

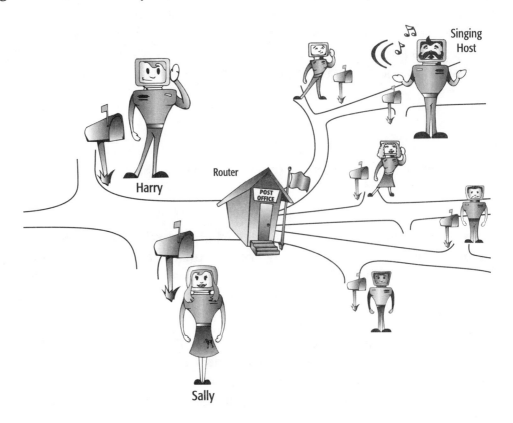

Some of the largest multimedia files that get transferred through the Internet include audio and video files. Streaming is a technique for transferring such data in a way that enables it to be processed as a steady and continuous flow. Without streaming, large multimedia files get broken up into smaller packets and reach end users in a hit-or-miss order. As the application is trying to display the data, the out-of-order pattern results in an unacceptable, choppy presentation.

Because of the growing popularity of the Internet and the demand for these large multimedia files to arrive in a smooth, orderly fashion, streaming technologies are becoming increasingly important. Most users do not have fast enough access to download large multimedia files quickly. With streaming, Web browsers can start displaying the data before the entire file has been transmitted.

In the streaming process, the host receiving the data collects the data and sends it up the protocol stack to the application that is processing the data. The application converts the data to sound or pictures and presents it as one smooth flow of information. If the host receiving the stream receives the data faster than it can be processed, that host needs to temporarily save the excess data in a buffer so that it can be presented by the application in a smooth manner. If the data isn't received quickly enough, though, the presentation of the data will not be smooth; it will be choppy and staticky.

Review Questions

1. List three other names for *hardware address*.

_____

_____

_____

2. What hardware address is a broadcast packet addressed to?

_____

3. List four protocols at the Internet layer.

_____

_____

_____

_____

4. List two responsibilities of IP.

_____

_____

5. What protocol resolves an IP address to a hardware address?

_____

6. How long will IP-to-hardware address resolution stay in ARP cache?

_____

7. What hardware address is an ARP request sent to?

_____

8. What hardware address is an ARP reply sent to?

_____

9. What software utility uses ICMP?

_____

10. What information is contained in an ARP request?

_____

11. What information is contained in an ARP reply?

_____

12. List three examples of a network topology.

_____

_____

_____

13. When is the hardware address assigned to the network interface card?

_____

14. How many characters does the hardware address contain?

_____

Terms to Know
❑ default gateway
❑ router
❑ routing table
❑ ARP
❑ resolve
❑ ARP cache
❑ ARP request
❑ ARP reply
❑ source-quench
❑ ping
❑ firewall
❑ stream
❑ reserved IP address
❑ multicast address

Chapter

4

The Transport Layer

The Transport layer determines whether the sender and the receiver will set up a connection before communicating and how often they will send acknowledgments of that connection to each other.

The Transport layer has only two protocols:

 Transmission Control Protocol (TCP)

 User Datagram Protocol (UDP)

Whereas TCP sets up a connection and sends acknowledgments, UDP does not. UDP can move data faster, but TCP guarantees delivery. Both are explained in this chapter.

Understanding the Transport Layer

The protocols at the Transport layer deliver data to and receive data from the Transport layer protocols of other hosts. The other host can be on the local network or on a network thousands of miles away. In some documentation, the Transport layer is also called the Host-to-Host layer.

The Transport layer of the TCP/IP protocol suite consists of only two protocols, TCP and UDP. TCP provides connection-oriented, reliable communication, and UDP provides connectionless, unreliable communication. TCP is slower and typically used for transferring large amounts of data to ensure that the data won't have to be sent again. UDP is faster and typically used for transferring small amounts of data.

Connection-oriented means that a connection is established as the communication begins. During this connection, certain information is exchanged to set the parameters of the main communication. Questions such as the following are answered:

- How much data can each host receive at a time?
- What sequence numbers should the hosts use in this connection?
- What acknowledgment numbers should be used in this connection?
- How long should each host wait for acknowledgments before resending data?

Reliable means that an acknowledgment will be sent back to the sending host throughout the communication to verify receipt of the packets. As each segment of data is received at the destination, an acknowledgment is sent to the sender within a specified period. If an acknowledgment is not sent within that time, the sender resends the data. If the receiver of the data gets the data in a damaged condition, the damaged packet is simply discarded. The recipient sends no acknowledgment for the damaged packet, and because the sender receives no acknowledgment, the data is re-sent.

The screen capture below shows the TCP portion of a packet. Notice the sequence and acknowledgment numbers: Frame 1 is sent from Harry to the FTP server to establish the connection; the sequence numbers are 2714368-2714371. Frame 2 is sent from the FTP server (and delivered by Harry's default gateway) and displays an acknowledgment for 2714369.

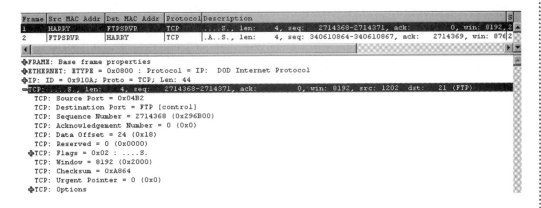

Unlike TCP, UDP provides connectionless, unreliable communication. *Connectionless* means that no connection is established before data transfer begins. The sending host does not send any setup packets to the destination; it just starts sending. This process is similar to the service that has an operator announcing the correct time when you call a designated telephone number. The operator continually sends out the current time; if nobody gets it, that's okay. The communication is considered unreliable because there will be no acknowledgments that the data was received at the destination. In addition, this type of packet contains a small header at the Transport layer, and because there is no connection to establish and no acknowledgment to wait for, data can be transferred faster.

The screen capture below shows the UDP portion of a packet. Notice that the UDP header is very small compared to the TCP portion of the packet shown above. The UDP portion has no sequence numbers nor acknowledgments. The packet is simply sent out, and hopefully the recipient gets it.

Understanding Transmission Control Protocol

Transmission Control Protocol (TCP) is the protocol that connects the sending host and the receiving host to each other. TCP is a **connection-oriented** protocol, which means that the two hosts that are communicating know about each other. One of the first aspects they determine is how to communicate with each other, where to send data, and how it will be received. The protocol guarantees delivery of packets by sending **acknowledgments** after each packet is received.

Before a sender begins sending data to a receiver, a short conversation takes place. The conversation is initiated by the TCP protocol at the Transport layer of the sending host. The protocol sends a packet to the receiving host to set up the communication for transferring data.

TCP is similar to the protocol for using a walkie-talkie. The first person tries to set up a connection by asking, "Hello, are you there?" The other person responds with, "Yes, I'm here, go ahead." Then a conversation begins, and every time one person gives some information, the other needs to respond with an acknowledgment that the information was received. Several times in the walkie-talkie conversation, the one receiving the information says, "Okay, got it, keep going."

Using a Three-Way Handshake

A conversation is started with a **three-way handshake**. In the first step of this process, the initiator of the conversation sends a packet to the other host requesting that they start a conversation. In the second step, the destination host sends back an acknowledgment that agrees to set up the communication and sets some parameters. In the final step, the initiator sends back one more packet that is a confirmation of the connection.

A good analogy for the three-way handshake is a secretary placing a call for an executive. The secretary acts like TCP when initiating the call for the executive. The secretary sets up the call with the destination executive and possibly lays down some guidelines. After the destination executive and the secretary have agreed, the "real" conversation begins between the executives.

The three-way handshake is used to set up TCP/IP communication, for example, when requesting a Web page. In the following dialog, Harry the Host is setting up a conversation with Wally the Web Server. The Web server is a host on the Internet that listens for requests and responds by sending Web pages. This is a sample of the process used to set up a conversation between any two hosts so that TCP/IP communication can occur.

> **Harry:** "Hello, I would like to connect to you and make some requests from you. Please send a packet to me to acknowledge that you received this. Please send it to my port 1076; that's where I'll be listening for your response."

> **Wally:** "Hi, I am acknowledging receipt of a packet from you. I would be happy to set up a connection with you. Please acknowledge that you received this packet."

> **Harry:** "All right, I'm acknowledging receipt of a packet from you. Thanks for acknowledging me. Let's get started."

In the illustration below, Harry the Host sets up communication with Wally the Web Server.

Then the conversation continues like this:

> **Harry:** "Hi, it's me. I'd like you to send me your home page."

> **Wally:** "Here's some of it. Let me know when you've got it, and I'll send you more."

> **Harry:** "Got it; let me have more."

> **Wally:** "Here's some more; let me know when you've got it."

---

three-way handshake
A three-step conversation initiated by TCP to set up a connection between hosts.

Organizing Data and Guaranteeing Delivery

TCP is a connection-oriented protocol because the connection is set up and used for the entire conversation. As packets are moved between the hosts having the conversation, TCP provides the connection. Each packet has a TCP header that includes **sequence numbers**, acknowledgment numbers, addresses, and other pieces of connection information.

TCP is also responsible for dividing the data into smaller packets if the data is too large to fit into a single packet. TCP on the destination host reassembles the packets so that the data is presented to the Application layer all put back together.

After a packet is sent, the sending host waits for an acknowledgment before sending more data. This is the feature of TCP that guarantees delivery of packets. If an acknowledgment is not received at the sending host, the sender resends the packet.

Every TCP packet that is received by the receiver triggers TCP to send back an acknowledgment packet. If the sending host does not receive the acknowledgment, then something must have gone wrong. Rather than send out a search-and-rescue party to try to find the packet, TCP on the host simply retransmits the missing packet.

Many times my wife tells me that she would like me to at least respond to something she is saying. I listen to her talk and instead of immediately responding, I think through what she's saying. Or maybe I just pretend to listen while I think about a baseball game, and I forget to respond. She says, "Are you listening to me?" What she wants is a response before she sends me more information. I could respond with a grunt or a nod of my head, and that would let her know that I received the data and I'm ready for more. Likewise, TCP would just like an acknowledgment before sending more data.

---

sequence numbers
Numbers in a header that indicate the order of packets. If packets get out of order en route to the destination host, this numbering system enables packets to be rearranged in order at the destination host.

Understanding User Datagram Protocol

User Datagram Protocol (UDP) is the protocol used at the Transport layer for **connectionless**, non-guaranteed communication. Unlike TCP, UDP does not set up a connection and does not use acknowledgments.

Instead, UDP just blasts out the packets. If the receiver gets the packet, great; if not, oh well. If a UDP packet gets lost or never arrives at the destination, the sender doesn't know nor care about it. When an application uses UDP, no connection gets set up before a conversation starts—the sender just sends.

In other words, UDP is similar to me teaching a class on television. I send out the data but I'm not waiting for you to acknowledge any of the data. It is not specifically going to anyone, but I'm hoping that you're watching. This communication method is much faster than teaching you in my classroom. In my classroom, I'd be looking for your acknowledgments before continuing to the next topic. On television, I don't have to wait; I'm hoping that you get it, but I don't know. As a matter of fact, you may have left the room to get a soda and a sandwich. Still, I keep on sending the data because I'm not waiting for your acknowledgments.

UDP is useful when TCP would be too complex, too slow, or just unnecessary.

UDP provides a few details in the UDP header that are used to get the packet to the right port at the destination host. One of the parameters in the small UDP header is the port number. The 16-bit UDP port number indicates the location of the service that the host is looking for.

Another value that is placed into the UDP header is a checksum. The sending host calculates the checksum by using a special algorithm and then places the checksum into the UDP header. The algorithm applies an equation to the data that is being sent (all the 1s and 0s). The checksum is used by the receiving host to verify that the packet was received intact. The recipient applies the same algorithm to the received packet, and if the value matches the UDP checksum value, the packet was received intact. If the values are different, the packet is simply discarded and ignored.

User Datagram Protocol (UDP)
A protocol offering a limited amount of service when messages are exchanged between hosts. No connection is set up and no acknowledgments are expected.

connectionless
Communication that occurs without a connection first being set up.

UDP Communication

In terms of computers, a host may use UDP to make a request of some service, not knowing where that service is located. A UDP conversation is similar to one Harry the Host might have when looking for a Dynamic Host Configuration Protocol (DHCP) server. He doesn't send a request to the DHCP server because he doesn't know where it is. There is no acknowledgment that anyone received the packet. However, Donna the DHCP server does hear his request and responds.

The short conversation would be like this:

> **Harry:** "Hey, I'm looking for a DHCP server."
>
> **Donna:** "I am a DHCP server."

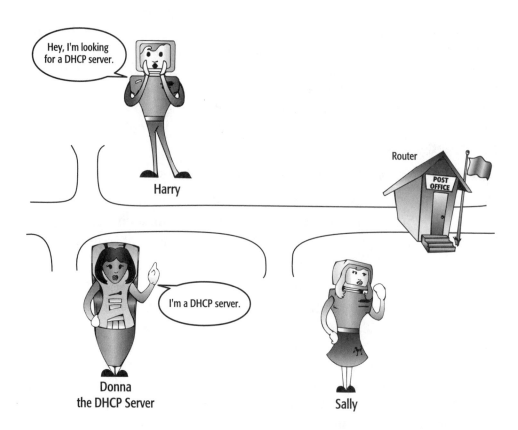

When Harry sends out the UDP packet, no connection is set up nor does Harry wait for an acknowledgment of packet receipt. Harry waits for the answer to the request, but not for an acknowledgment.

When UDP is used, the connection and guarantee of the packets are usually the responsibility of a higher layer. The application that resides at a higher layer is responsible for making sure that the UDP packets are getting to their destinations correctly.

Throughout this chapter you have learned the differences between TCP and UDP. One of the most striking comparisons is the size of the header at the Transport layer.

The screen capture below is the layout of the TCP header from the actual RFC in which TCP is described. RFC 761 details TCP; here is the author's header description:

```
TCP Header Format

 0                   1                   2                   3
 0 1 2 3 4 5 6 7 8 9 0 1 2 3 4 5 6 7 8 9 0 1 2 3 4 5 6 7 8 9 0 1
+-+-+-+-+-+-+-+-+-+-+-+-+-+-+-+-+-+-+-+-+-+-+-+-+-+-+-+-+-+-+-+-+
|          Source Port          |       Destination Port        |
+-+-+-+-+-+-+-+-+-+-+-+-+-+-+-+-+-+-+-+-+-+-+-+-+-+-+-+-+-+-+-+-+
|                        Sequence Number                        |
+-+-+-+-+-+-+-+-+-+-+-+-+-+-+-+-+-+-+-+-+-+-+-+-+-+-+-+-+-+-+-+-+
|                     Acknowledgment Number                     |
+-+-+-+-+-+-+-+-+-+-+-+-+-+-+-+-+-+-+-+-+-+-+-+-+-+-+-+-+-+-+-+-+
| Data  |           |U|A|E|R|S|F|                                |
| Offset| Reserved  |R|C|O|S|Y|I|            Window              |
|       |           |G|K|L|T|N|N|                                |
+-+-+-+-+-+-+-+-+-+-+-+-+-+-+-+-+-+-+-+-+-+-+-+-+-+-+-+-+-+-+-+-+
|           Checksum            |         Urgent Pointer        |
+-+-+-+-+-+-+-+-+-+-+-+-+-+-+-+-+-+-+-+-+-+-+-+-+-+-+-+-+-+-+-+-+
|                    Options                    |    Padding     |
+-+-+-+-+-+-+-+-+-+-+-+-+-+-+-+-+-+-+-+-+-+-+-+-+-+-+-+-+-+-+-+-+
|                             data                              |
+-+-+-+-+-+-+-+-+-+-+-+-+-+-+-+-+-+-+-+-+-+-+-+-+-+-+-+-+-+-+-+-+

                        TCP Header Format
```

Notice how large and complicated this header looks.

Compare the TCP header to the simple, relatively small header of UDP, which is detailed in RFC 768.

```
 0      7 8     15 16    23 24    31
+--------+--------+--------+--------+
|     Source      |   Destination   |
|     Port        |      Port       |
+--------+--------+--------+--------+
|                 |                 |
|     Length      |    Checksum     |
+--------+--------+--------+--------+
|
|        data octets ...
+--------------- ...

         User Datagram Header Format
```

Review Questions

Terms to Know
- ❏ TCP
- ❏ connection-oriented
- ❏ acknowledgments
- ❏ three-way handshake
- ❏ sequence numbers
- ❏ UDP
- ❏ connectionless

1. List the two protocols at the Transport layer.

_____

_____

2. List two important characteristics of each protocol.

_____

_____

3. What is the name of the process that TCP uses to set up a connection?

_____

4. What does TCP at the destination host send back to the sending host after receiving data?

_____

5. How long will UDP on the sending host wait for an acknowledgment before sending more data?

_____

6. When UDP is used, what is responsible for the guarantee of packet delivery?

_____

7. What is the benefit of UDP?

_____

8. What is the benefit of TCP?

_____

9. Which RFC describes TCP?

_____

10. Which RFC describes UDP?

_____

11. Which protocol uses a larger header, TCP or UDP?

_____

12. What is the purpose of a checksum?

_____

Chapter

5

The Application Layer

At the top of the TCP/IP stack is the Application layer. The Application layer contains applications that process requests from other hosts. Ports and sockets are used to receive and send data. To best describe the Application layer, this chapter closely examines the following topics:

 Ports and sockets

 File Transfer Protocol (FTP)

 Hypertext Transfer Protocol (HTTP)

Understanding the Application Layer

Application layer
The top layer of the DoD and OSI models where applications listen for and respond to requests.

ports
Numbered addresses where requests are sent and where applications listen for requests. Ports are numbered 1–65,536.

The **Application layer** is the part of the TCP/IP where requests for data or services are processed. Applications at this layer are waiting for requests to process and they are all listening at their respective **ports**.

The Application layer is not where your word processor, spreadsheet, or Internet browser application is running. Applications that are running at the Application layer interact with the word processor, spreadsheet, or Internet browser application. Two examples of applications that run at the Application layer are FTP and HTTP. Both are detailed later in this chapter.

Understanding Ports and Sockets

As a packet is moving up through the stack on its way to the Application layer, the Transport layer directs the packet to the appropriate port. A port is a number that the application at the Application layer uses as a send-and-receive address. A port is like a stereo speaker, and applications are set up to listen at a particular speaker. The application puts its ear to the speaker and waits for a request to be passed through it.

Imagine that the application is listening for requests to process. As a request makes its way up the TCP/IP stack, either TCP or UDP at the Transport layer hands the request up to the application. Remember, the application is set up to listen at a specific port number, and TCP or UDP sends the request to the appropriate port based on information in the packet's header.

As a good analogy, imagine a local fast-food restaurant, which is a combination of a popular hamburger franchise and a popular seafood franchise. When I order the Number 1 Value Meal, how do the employees know which Number 1 Value Meal I mean? Do I mean the hamburger or seafood Number 1? What kind of burger or fish is the Number 1?

I specify that I want the hamburger restaurant's Number 1 Value Meal when I place the order. The employee behind the counter documents the order and passes it to the appropriate cook. Both the hamburger and the seafood cooks have a different meaning for *Number 1 Value Meal*, and depending on which cook the order is passed to, I get a burger or fish. Based on it being a Number *1* Value Meal, the cook knows which burger to cook or fish to fry.

Note that when I order a Number 1 Value Meal, instead of saying the name of the burger, fries, and soda, I just say "Hamburger Number 1." The employee at the counter then knows which cook to pass my order to so that it can be processed. Similarly, rather than specify the name of an application to get passed to, the packet specifies the port number to get passed to.

TCP and UDP have use of 65,536 ports each. A packet, for example, may specify that it is bound for TCP port 80. TCP port 80 is the standard port for Web servers to listen for HTTP requests. As another example, a packet may specify that it is bound for UDP port 69, which is the standard for TFTP requests. The Internet layer passed this packet to either TCP or UDP and now TCP or UDP at the Transport layer passes the packet to the appropriate port where the application is listening for requests.

socket
IP address : TCP or UDP : port number.

Think of this port information forming a funnel through the TCP/IP stack. As soon as a packet is delivered to a particular IP address, it is passed up through the stack to make sure it is addressed to the host that received it. Then it is passed up to TCP or UDP and then to the appropriate port so that the application at the Application layer can process the request. This funnel is called a **socket**.

A socket combines three pieces of information: the IP address, TCP or UDP, and the port number. The TCP or UDP indicates which protocol is to be used. A socket is written like this:

131.107.2.200:TCP:80 or 131.107.2.200:UDP:69

The illustration below shows the TCP/IP protocol stack with 65,536 TCP ports and 65,536 UDP ports at the Application layer. Notice that as a packet moves up the stack, IP will direct the packet to the either a TCP port or a UDP port. The applications are listening at their appropriate ports so that when data arrives, it can be processed accurately.

Well-Known Ports

Well-known ports are port numbers that the **Internet Assigned Number Authority (IANA)** has reserved for specific applications to use. For example:

well-known ports
Port numbers 1–1,024, which are reserved for certain applications.

Internet Assigned Numbers Authority (IANA)
An organization responsible for overseeing several aspects of the Internet.

Port	Reserved For
TCP:80	HTTP
TCP:21	FTP
TCP:20	FTP-Data
UDP:69	Trivial File Transfer Protocol (TFTP)
UDP:161	Simple Network Management Protocol (SNMP)

The port numbers between 1 and 1,024 are considered well-known port numbers and are reserved for specified applications, just as 911 and 411 are reserved and well-known telephone numbers. Port numbers between 1,025 and 65,536 have no specified use. Programmers use these ports for new applications they are writing. Well-known ports were originally documented in RFC 1060 and were updated in RFC 1700.

The illustration below shows Harry the Host sending a request to Wally the Web Server, who is listening to requests from a few different ports. Harry sends a request to TCP port 80, requesting that Wally send him a Web page.

File Transfer Protocol (FTP)

File Transfer Protocol (FTP) is the protocol that defines how a file can be transferred from one host to another. For a file to be transferred from one host to another, the FTP on the initiating host creates the request for a file, and FTP on the FTP server processes the requests for a file. A programmer who would like to learn all of the idiosyncrasies of FTP should read RFC 959.

Two hosts are involved in an FTP session. One host requests a file, and the other host has a copy of the file and transfers a copy to the requesting host. Files can be transferred in either a text or **binary format**.

The host that is requesting the service is called a client and the host that provides the service is called a server. These two hosts establish a client/server relationship, which is simply one host making requests of another.

The requesting host uses an application to request the file. The application may be a word processor, an **FTP command line utility,** or an **FTP command interpreter**. The FTP command line utility enables a host to connect to an **FTP server** without using a fancy interface by having the user simply enter FTP commands at the command line. FTP connects to the FTP server, and the user is requested to log in. The user must supply a username and a password. In the screen capture below, a connection was made to an FTP server at ftp.microsoft.com. In this FTP session, the user logged in with the account name ftp and no password.

```
C:\>ftp ftp.microsoft.com
Connected to ftp.microsoft.com.
220 CPMSFTFTPA04 Microsoft FTP Service (Version 5.0).
User (ftp.microsoft.com:(none)): ftp
331 Anonymous access allowed, send identity (e-mail name) as password.
Password:
230-This is FTP.MICROSOFT.COM. Please see the dirmap.txt file for more information.
230 Anonymous user logged in.
ftp>
```

TIP

Most FTP sites will allow an **anonymous** user to log in with no password. When prompted for a username, you can type **anonymous**. However, because *anonymous* is so difficult to spell, you might want to log in by typing **ftp** as your anonymous username. Although no password is required, using your e-mail address as a password is considered "good FTP etiquette" when using the anonymous account.

File Transfer Protocol (FTP)
An application used to transfer files from one host to another and to store the files on the requesting host.

---

binary format
A compressed file format.

FTP command line utility
A non-mouse and non-fancy interface used to access an FTP server.

FTP command interpreter
A nice looking, easy-to-use application used to access an FTP server.

FTP server
Server on which an FTP server application is running to transfer files out to clients.

---

anonymous
Account set up so that anyone can access files on an FTP server without a secret password.

How FTP Works

The first packet that is sent from the requesting host to the FTP server is a TCP/IP packet requesting to set up a connection. In this example, the packet was sent to TCP port 21 on the FTP server. The requesting host chose a non-well-known port to listen for the reply. In this case, the requesting host chose 1177 as the return port and will be listening for a response sent to that port number. In the next screen capture, the first TCP/IP packet is shown as the requesting host makes a request from the source port of 1177 to destination port of 21.

Frame	Src MAC Addr	Dst MAC Addr	Protocol	Description
2356	Harry's Default Gateway	HARRY	FTP	Resp. to Port 1177, '230 Anonymous user logged i
2357	HARRY	Harry's Default Gateway	TCP	.A...., len: 0, seq: 2218581-2218581, ack:1

```
⊕FRAME: Base frame properties
⊕ETHERNET: ETYPE = 0x0800 : Protocol = IP:  DOD Internet Protocol
⊕IP: ID = 0xC104; Proto = TCP; Len: 40
=TCP: .A...., len:    0, seq:   2218581-2218581, ack:1654872938, win: 8516, src: 1177  dst:   21 (FTP)
   TCP: Source Port = 0x0499
   TCP: Destination Port = FTP [control]
   TCP: Sequence Number = 2218581 (0x21DA55)
   TCP: Acknowledgement Number = 1654872938 (0x62A35B6A)
   TCP: Data Offset = 20 (0x14)
   TCP: Reserved = 0 (0x0000)
 ⊕TCP: Flags = 0x10 : .A....
   TCP: Window = 8516 (0x2144)
   TCP: Checksum = 0x6CA1
   TCP: Urgent Pointer = 0 (0x0)
```

The FTP application was listening at port 21. Upon receiving the request, the application sent back an **FTP/TCP/IP** packet to set up the connection and ask that the client send back the username to log in. In this return packet, the FTP server is the source, and the FTP client is the destination. The FTP server sends this reply to port 1177, where the FTP client said it would be listening. In the FTP header that the FTP server built, the FTP server is passing FTP information to the FTP client.

Notice in the screen capture that the source port labeled src: is set to port 1177. Harry, the requesting host, has decided that the FTP server should send data back to this port.

The following screen capture shows the next packet in the sequence, where the FTP server replies to the FTP client.

Frame	Src MAC Addr	Dst MAC Addr	Protocol	Description
2355	HARRY	Harry's Default Gateway	TCP	.A...., len: 0, seq: 2218581-2218581, ack:1
2356	Harry's Default Gateway	HARRY	FTP	Resp. to Port 1177, '230 Anonymous user logged i

```
⊕FRAME: Base frame properties
⊕ETHERNET: ETYPE = 0x0800 : Protocol = IP:  DOD Internet Protocol
⊕IP: ID = 0xBE4A; Proto = TCP; Len: 71
⊕TCP: .AP..., len:   31, seq:1654872907-1654872937, ack:   2218581, win:17503, src:   21 (FTP)  dst: 1177
=FTP: Resp. to Port 1177, '230 Anonymous user logged in.'
   FTP: FTP Error Return Code = 230
   FTP: FTP Command Arg1 = Anonymous
   FTP: FTP Data: Number of data bytes remaining = 18 (0x0012)
```

This dialog continues as the FTP server responds to the FTP client's requests. The client will be able to see a list of files that are available and request either one or more server files be transferred.

The command-line FTP client application requires that the user know the FTP commands and how to use them. Another way that the user can connect to an FTP server—without knowing how to use the commands—is to use an FTP command interpreter. Several of these interpreter applications are available on the Internet; some are shareware and some can be downloaded and used for a trial period. An example of one that can be downloaded for a 30-day trial before you buy it is **CuteFTP**. CuteFTP has an easy-to-learn and easy-to-use interface. This client application interprets the user's clicks, translates them to FTP commands, and passes those commands to the FTP server. Another example of an FTP command interpreter available on the Internet is FTP Voyager.

CuteFTP
An easy-to-use FTP command interpreter application that turns your mouse clicks into FTP commands.

TIP

For FTP to work, the server must be running an FTP server application, and the client must be using an FTP client application.

Hypertext Transfer Protocol (HTTP)

Hypertext Transfer Protocol (HTTP)
An application used to transfer files from one host to another and to display the files at the requesting host.

Web server
Server on which an HTTP server application is running that users can surf to and request files be transferred and displayed.

Web browser application
A client application used for surfing the Web. Examples are Netscape Navigator and Microsoft Internet Explorer.

Uniform Resource Locator (URL)
The address of the Web site that the user is surfing to.

Hypertext Transfer Protocol (HTTP) is a set of rules for exchanging files on the Internet. This is the protocol that your Web browser uses when surfing the Internet. Unlike FTP, HTTP is designed so that very little user intervention is required. HTTP transfers preformatted files that are displayed in their browser instead of just saved to disk. The HTTP application runs on a **Web server** and listens for requests, and then responds by sending files back to the requestor. A Web server is a server that has the HTTP service application running on it. HTTP listens at a TCP port, usually port 80 for requests, and then transfers the requested file back to the requestor. The requesting host displays the file in a **Web browser application**.

The client makes the HTTP request by issuing a command to their Web browser. The command is initiated by typing a **Uniform Resource Locator (URL)**, (such as www.sybex.com) in the address line of the Web browser or by clicking a **hyperlink** on a page that is being displayed by the Web browser. The Web browser formats the client's request into an **HTTP/TCP/IP** request packet with a destination port of 80.

At the Web server, the HTTP application is listening at port 80 for any requests. After the packet is received, the appropriate file is retrieved and packaged for delivery to the client. The packets leave the Web server, and upon arrival at the client, the Web browser decodes the **Hypertext Markup Language (HTML)** file and displays it onscreen with the proper formatting.

So, let's look at what is really happening when you connect to a Web site:

1. You open your Web browser and type in the URL **www.sybex.com**.

2. Your Web browser creates the TCP/IP packet and sends it to a Web server somewhere on the Internet. In other words, little ol' you makes a request of a big Web server to set up a connection.

3. The Web server hears your request at port 80 and sends back a packet to you that says, "Okay, I'll set up a connection with you."

4. Now that you have a connection with the Web server, you request that the Web server send you its default page.

5. The Web server receives your response and gets the file that you requested. The file is put into one or more packets, depending on how big the file is, and it is sent to you.

9. Why would an administrator change the HTTP port on the Web server to a port number other than 80?

_____

10. Which agency controls the well-known port assignments?

_____

11. What is the standard HTTP port?

_____

12. What are the three pieces of information that make up a socket?

_____

_____

_____

13. What is an FTP command line interpreter?

_____

Chapter
6

IP Addressing

This chapter covers Internet Protocol (IP) addresses. You will learn what an IP address is, how to distinguish valid from invalid IP addresses, and how all the available IP addresses are divided into categories called classes.

In this discussion of IP addresses, you will learn about the following:

 Binary and decimal numbering systems

 Binary-to-decimal and decimal-to-binary conversions

 The five classes of IP addresses

What Is IP Addressing?

Every host on a TCP/IP network needs to have a unique address, similar to you needing a unique address for your house. With this unique address, it is possible to send data from host to host. Every packet contains addressing information in the header, and the IP address in the header is used to route packets. If several people on your street had the same address, the post office would have a difficult time sorting mail. For a similar reason, IP addresses are unique on each network.

IP addressing is simply configuring each TCP/IP host with a valid IP address. For access to the Internet, a host must have an IP address that identifies not only the host address (like a house number) but also identifies the network address (like a street number). An administrator needs to be aware of proper addressing techniques so that the hosts on the network will function correctly.

Numbering Systems

An IP address uniquely identifies every host on a network. Just as your mailing address uniquely identifies your home, an IP address uniquely identifies a host.

Consider that your mailing address is made up of two parts. Part of it tells the postal carrier what street you live on and part of it tells the post office which house you live in on that street. All addresses on your street include the same street name but have a unique number for each house. IP addresses are similar: They can be broken down into two parts. One part of the IP address represents the network that the host is on, and the other part represents that unique host on that network.

TCP/IP looks at IP addresses in **binary** form, but as humans, we prefer to see IP addresses in **decimal** form. Because the protocol is seeing only binary, working with IP addresses makes more sense when you also look at the IP addresses in binary. To do so, you need to understand the two numbering systems and be able to convert from one to another.

binary

The base-2 number system that computers use to represent data. It consists of only two digits: 0 and 1.

decimal

The base-10 number system that people use to represent data. It consists of 10 digits: 0, 1, 2, 3, 4, 5, 6, 7, 8, 9.

The decimal numbering system uses the digits 0, 1, 2, 3, 4, 5, 6, 7, 8, and 9. In the binary numbering system, the only digits that exist are 0 and 1.

To better understand the binary numbering system, let's take a closer look at the decimal numbering system that you are already familiar with. When you analyze the decimal numbering system, it is clear that the numbers represent a specific value depending on which place, or column, the number is in. For example, the number 27 has a 2 in the tens column and a 7 in the ones column. The resulting value is $(2 \times 10) + (7 \times 1)$.

As you scan across a decimal number, the value of the digit in each column increases from right to left. The value of the digit in the rightmost column results from multiplying the number by 1. The value of the digit in the next column to the left is found by multiplying the number by 10, the next column to the left by 100, and the next by 1,000. The value of the columns continues to increase by a factor of 10 as you move to the left. After you have found the value of each of the columns, you add the values together to obtain the value of the overall number.

You increment numbers in the decimal and binary systems in the same way. In either system, you continue to increase the rightmost digit by 1 until you reach the highest value in the numbering system (that is, until you reach 9 in the decimal system or until you reach 1 in the binary system). After you have reached the highest value, add 1 to the digit immediately to the left and start the rightmost digit from the lowest value again.

For example: In the decimal number 321, 1 is the rightmost digit. To increment 321, add 1 to the rightmost digit to get 322. Continue increasing the rightmost digit by 1 until the rightmost digit holds the highest value: 329. Now increment the digit to the left and start the rightmost digit over from the lowest value: 330. After the highest digit is reached in the rightmost column, increase the digit in the next left column by 1. Then begin again, increasing the rightmost digit starting from 0.

NOTE

The octal and hexadecimal numbering systems are also used often in the computer industry. Octal is base-8 and hexadecimal is base-16.

Reviewing Binary and Decimal Numbering Systems

In the chart of decimal numbers below, notice that each number is represented by four digits. In the left column of the chart, the number 0000 is incremented by one until the value of 0009 is reached. At this point, the ones place has reached the highest value of the numbering system so the digit in the tens place is incremented and the value in the ones place begins again from 0010. Each of the chart's columns shows the four-digit number being incremented by 1 until the 9 is reached.

Each group of three columns represents a point in the decimal numbering system where incrementing the rightmost value causes the next column to be incremented.

0000	0010	0020	...	0090	0100	0110	...	0990	1000	1010
0001	0011	0021		0091	0101	0111		0991	1001	1011
0002	0012	0022		0092	0102	0112		0992	1002	1012
0003	0013	0023		0093	0103	0113		0993	1003	1013
0004	0014	0024		0094	0104	0114		0994	1004	1014
0005	0015	0025		0095	0105	0115		0995	1005	1015
0006	0016	0026		0096	0106	0116		0996	1006	1016
0007	0017	0027		0097	0107	0117		0997	1007	1017
0008	0018	0028		0098	0108	0118		0998	1008	1018
0009	0019	0029		0099	0109	0119		0999	1009	1019

The binary numbering system works the same way except you can use only 1s and 0s. Therefore, every time that you increment by 1, you have reached the highest value in the binary numbering system. The following chart shows four binary digits being incremented by 1.

0000	1000
0001	1001
0010	1010
0011	1011
0100	1100
0101	1101
0110	1110
0111	1111

Converting Binary Numbers to Decimal

TCP/IP always uses binary IP addresses. But people tend to use decimal IP addresses because we can more easily work with this familiar form. Converting binary to decimal and decimal to binary is an important skill enabling network administrators to know the exact values that TCP/IP uses.

TEST IT OUT: CONVERT FROM BINARY TO DECIMAL

To convert binary to decimal, first examine the binary digits. For each column that has a 1, note its decimal value, and then add those values together to get the decimal equivalent. The decimal values for each column remain constant:

- ◇ The rightmost column has a decimal value of 1.
- ◇ The second column from the right has a decimal value of 2.
- ◇ The third column from the right has a decimal value of 4.
- ◇ The fourth column from the right has a decimal value of 8.

So, for example, in the binary number 0011, you have 1s in two columns. You know that the rightmost column has the decimal value of 1, and the second column from the right has the decimal value of 2. Add 1 and 2 and you get 3. Therefore, the decimal equivalent of 0011 is 3.

Now try the following examples:

1. Convert the binary number 0001.

    The decimal equation for the conversion is 0 + 0 + 0 + 1

    = 1 decimal

2. Convert the binary number 0110.

    The decimal equation for the conversion is 0 + 4 + 2 + 0

    = 6 decimal

3. Convert the binary number 1110.

    The decimal equation for the conversion is 8 + 4 + 2 + 0

    = 14 decimal

4. Convert the binary number 1111.

    The decimal equation for the conversion is 8 + 4 + 2 + 1

    = 15 decimal

Each of these columns represents a bit (*bi*nary dig*it*). The greatest decimal number that can be represented by four bits is 15.

Converting Decimal Numbers to Binary

Several simple methods can be used to convert decimal numbers to binary. Find one that you are comfortable with, practice it and you'll get the hang of it. Presented in this section are a few methods that you might find useful.

Using the Bit Value Method

One method of converting a decimal number to binary is the opposite of converting binary to decimal. First, you find the binary position with the greatest decimal value that is still less than the number that you are converting. Give a value of 1 for that binary position, subtract the bit value from the original decimal number, and repeat the process for the remainder.

 TEST IT OUT: CONVERT FROM DECIMAL TO BINARY

To convert the decimal value 9 to binary by using the bit value method, start with a binary chart like the following:

x	x	x	x
8	4	2	1

You can see that the binary position with the greatest decimal value that is still less than 9 is the 8-bit. So you put a 1 in the 8-bit, subtract the bit value (8) from the original number (9), and you have a remainder of 1.

1	x	x	x =	8, and 9 – 8 leaves a remainder of 1
8	4	2	1	

You repeat the process with the remainder: The largest binary position that has a value less than 1 is the 1-bit. Put a 1 in the 1-bit. Because you have no remainder, the rest of the bits are 0s and you are finished.

1	0	0	1 =	9, and 9 – 9 leaves a remainder of 0
8	4	2	1	

So, the decimal value 9 is 1001 in binary.

Now, try these examples:

1. Convert the decimal value 6 to binary.

	x	x	x	x	
	8	4	2	1	
Result:	0	1	1	0 =	6 (0 + 4 + 2 + 0)

TEST IT OUT: CONVERT FROM DECIMAL TO BINARY (cont.)

2. Convert the decimal value 11 to binary.

x	x	x	x		
8	4	2	1		
Result: 1	0	1	1 =	3 (8 + 0 + 2 + 1)	

3. Convert the decimal value 3 to binary.

x	x	x	x		
8	4	2	1		
Result: 0	0	1	1 =	11 (0 + 0 + 2 + 1)	

4. Convert the decimal value 15 to binary.

x	x	x	x		
8	4	2	1		
Result: 1	1	1	1 =	15 (8 + 4 + 2 + 1)	

5. Convert the decimal value 8 to binary.

x	x	x	x		
8	4	2	1		
Result: 1	0	0	0 =	8 (8 + 0 + 0 + 0)	

6. Convert the decimal value 9 to binary.

x	x	x	x		
8	4	2	1		
Result: 1	0	0	1 =	9 (8 + 0 + 0 + 1)	

7. Convert the decimal value 5 to binary.

x	x	x	x		
8	4	2	1		
Result: 0	1	0	1 =	5 (0 + 4 + 0 + 1)	

8. Convert the decimal value 13 to binary.

x	x	x	x		
8	4	2	1		
Result: 1	1	0	1 =	13 (8 + 4 + 0 + 1)	

Using the Division Method

Another method of converting decimal numbers to binary is called the division method. The division method uses a series of simple divide-by-2 problems to complete the conversion. Every time you divide by 2, the remainder will be either 1 or 0. It is important to list the remainders (whether a 1 or a 0) in an orderly fashion because the binary result will be comprised of these remainders.

The process is as follows:

1. Divide the decimal number by 2 and write the remainder, 1 or 0.
2. Divide the quotient (answer) by 2 and write that remainder, 1 or 0.
3. Repeat steps 1 and 2 until the quotient is 0.
4. Write the remainders in reverse order for the binary equivalent.

 TEST IT OUT: CONVERT FROM DECIMAL TO BINARY USING THE DIVISION METHOD

Follow this example step-by-step and then try using the division method to complete the next conversion problems. To convert the decimal value 6 to binary:

1. Divide 6 by 2 (6/2 = 3 with a remainder of 0). Write 0 as the first remainder.
2. Divide the quotient, 3, by 2. (3/2 = 1 remainder of 1). Write 1 as the second remainder.
3. Divide the quotient, 1, by 2. (1/2 = 0 remainder of 1). Write 1 as the third remainder. The quotient is now 0 so you don't have to repeat the previous steps.
4. Note that the remainders are 011. Reverse them to get the binary number 110.

Now try the following examples:

1. Convert the decimal value 11 to binary.

    11/2 = 5 remainder of 1

    5/2 = 2 remainder of 1

    2/2 = 1 remainder of 0

    1/2 = 0 remainder of 1

    Result: 1011

TEST IT OUT: CONVERT FROM DECIMAL TO BINARY USING THE DIVISION METHOD (cont.)

2. Convert the decimal value 15 to binary.

$15/2 = 7$ remainder of 1

$7/2 = 3$ remainder of 1

$3/2 = 1$ remainder of 1

$1/2 = 0$ remainder of 1

Result: 1111

3. Convert the decimal value 4 to binary

$4/2 = 2$ remainder of 0

$2/2 = 1$ remainder of 0

$1/2 = 0$ remainder of 1

Result 100

4. Convert the decimal value 10 to binary

$10/2 = 5$ remainder of 0

$5/2 = 2$ remainder of 1

$2/2 = 1$ remainder of 0

$1/2 = 0$ remainder of 1

Result 1010

5. Convert the decimal value 7 to binary

$7/2 = 3$ remainder of 1

$3/2 = 1$ remainder of 1

$1/2 = 0$ remainder of 1

Result 111

Using a Calculator

One other method of converting either decimal to binary or binary to decimal is to use a calculator. It is important that you understand the math behind converting numbers between the numbering systems, but most administrators end up using a calculator because it is quicker and easier to avoid mistakes.

The most common calculator is the electronic calculator that is installed with all the Microsoft desktop operating systems. The calculator has not changed much from Windows 95, 98, or NT. You can access the calculator by clicking Start ➢ Programs ➢ Accessories ➢ Calculator. A screen shot of the calculator is shown below.

TIP

Be sure the calculator is in the Scientific mode by clicking View ➢ Scientific.

After you are sure the calculator is in Scientific view, notice the row of radio buttons on the upper-left side. The Dec button puts the calculator into decimal mode, and the Bin button puts the calculator into binary mode. To do any conversions, type in the number that you would like to convert, then click the radio button that is not selected. The number displayed is the converted number.

WARNING

When using a calculator to convert decimal numbers to binary, pay close attention to leading 0s getting dropped. For example, the decimal number 7 is displayed as 111 on a binary calculator. But when working with IP addresses, you'll generally want to use four or eight bits. The number 7 expressed with four bits is 0111 and with eight bits is 0000 0111. A calculator does not display the leading 0s because they are considered insignificant.

IP Addresses

TCP/IP addresses are based on 32-bit addresses. But rather than working with 32 ones and zeros, people use decimals to represent IP addresses—specifically, they use four decimal numbers separated by periods. These four decimal numbers represent the 32 binary digits separated into four equal parts called octets. An **octet** is eight bits.

An IP address expressed in decimal is referred to as **dotted decimal notation** because it has four decimal numbers, each separated by a period, or a dot. As I've stated, each of the four decimal numbers represents eight binary digits, or bits. In the preceding conversion examples, you looked only at four-bit binary numbers. In eight-bit numbers, the decimal values of the bits continue increasing from right to left:

- The fifth bit has a decimal value of 16.
- The sixth bit has a decimal value of 32.
- The seventh bit has a decimal value of 64.
- The eighth bit has a decimal value of 128.

128	64	32	16	8	4	2	1
x	x	x	x	x	x	x	x

So, for example, the binary number 0101 0101 is equal to the decimal 85:

$$0 + 64 + 0 + 16 + 0 + 4 + 0 + 1 = 85$$

The binary number 1001 0101 is equal to the decimal 145:

$$128 + 0 + 0 + 16 + 0 + 4 + 0 + 1 = 145$$

The binary number 1111 1111 is equal to the decimal 255:

$$128 + 64 + 32 + 16 + 8 + 4 + 2 + 1 = 255$$

octet
Eight bits of data.

dotted decimal notation
An IP address presented as four decimal numbers, each separated by a period, or dot.

The highest decimal number that an octet can contain is 255. The decimal number 256 cannot be represented with eight bits; therefore, no IP address has a number greater then 255 in any octet.

TCP/IP uses all 32 bits; therefore, it is important when you look at the four decimal numbers to understand that there are really 32 bits that TCP/IP is using. For example, the IP address 131.107.2.200 can be translated into the following binary octets:

131	=	1000 0011
107	=	0110 1011
2	=	0000 0010
200	=	1100 1000

Therefore, TCP/IP will see 131.107.2.200 as this:

    10000011011010110000001011001000

To humans, seeing all 32 bits is a little overwhelming, so obviously using the decimal equivalent is easier. When looking at the binary, most people separate each set of four bits so that all the 1s and 0s don't run together.

For example, the IP address 209.132.95.62 would be:

209	=	1101 0001
132	=	1000 0100
95	=	0101 1111
62	=	0011 1110

TCP/IP will see 209.132.95.62 as this:

    1101 0001 1000 0100 0101 1111 0011 1110

Some sample IP addresses are:

    15.231.25.115
    1.26.251.32
    221.26.0.1
    209.132.95.3

IP Address Classes

IP addresses are divided into five classes: Class A, Class B, Class C, Class D, and Class E. All addresses are placed in a particular class based on the decimal values of their first octets. In the first octet, an IP address can start with a decimal value between 1 and 255.

The system of class addresses has been set up to help ensure assignment of unique IP addresses. Let's take a look at how these classes are divided and who gets the IP addresses in each category.

Class A Addresses

Class A addresses have first octets with a decimal number between 1 and 127. For example:

```
1.x.y.z
10.x.y.z
27.x.y.z
102.x.y.z
```

In binary, a Class A address always starts with 0 as the leftmost bit. For example:

```
1.x.y.z    =    0000 0001.x.y.z
10.x.y.z   =    0000 0110.x.y.z
27.x.y.z   =    0001 1011.x.y.z
102.x.y.z  =    0110 0110.x.y.z
127.x.y.z  =    0111 1111.x.y.z
```

Notice that 127 has a 1 in every bit of the octet except the first bit. The next higher binary value will put a 1 in the leftmost bit, and the resulting address will not be a Class A. Therefore, 127.*x.y.z* is the highest Class A address.

Class A addresses use the first octet to represent the unique network address and leave three octets to develop unique host addresses on that network. Because there is a 0 in the first bit, the following seven bits in the first octet are used to distinguish the network from all other networks, and 24 bits are used by each host to make itself unique on the network. An important rule to note here is that a network address cannot have all 0s.

This means that there are only 127 Class A networks available. At first glance, it seems obvious that there are 127 networks, but the following equation proves the number:

$$2^7 - 1 = 127$$

where 2 is the number of possible values that each bit can contain (a 1 or a 0), 7 is the number of bits used, and 1 is the address where all 7 bits are 0 (you cannot have a network address of all 0s).

On each of those 127 networks, each address uses the other 24 bits to make itself unique. All possible combinations of these 24 bits make up the number of unique host IP addresses that can be on each of those 127 networks. There are 16,777,214 possible unique IP addresses on each of the 127 Class A networks. Similar to the rule that the network portion of the address cannot be all 0s, the host portion of the address cannot be all 0s and it cannot be all 1s. A host portion with all 1s refers to an IP broadcast address, which you learn about in a later chapter, and the host portion with all 0s is a reference to the network. Therefore, the equation for the number of hosts on each Class A network is:

$$2^{24} - 2 = 16,777,214$$

You subtract 2 because addresses with all 0s and all 1s are invalid.

Of the 127 Class A networks available, one address was reserved for testing: The network address 127.x.y.z was reserved as a **loopback** address. No host can ever use 127-dot-anything as its address because it has been reserved for diagnostic purposes. When testing a TCP/IP installation, 127-dot-anything refers to that TCP/IP installation. Therefore, for example, as a network administrator is testing a TCP/IP installation, testing 127.0.0.1 refers to the host that is being tested.

Addresses Reserved for Private Use

Certain addresses have been set aside by the InterNIC and reserved for private use only. If you would like to use TCP/IP on your internal network (intranet), and not use the Internet, the following addresses are suggested:

Class A   10.0.0.0 through 10.255.255.255

Class B   172.16.0.0 through 172.31.255.255

Class C   192.168.0.0 through 192.168.255.255

Routers on the Internet will not route data from or to these addresses; they are for internal, private use only. To use these addresses on an intranet and have access to the Internet, you must use a **proxy server** or **Network Address Translation (NAT)**.

---

loopback
An address that is used for diagnostic purposes, to test the TCP/IP stack of a TCP/IP host.

Proxy server
An application that relays TCP/IP traffic from one network to another while changing the IP address of the sending host.

Network Address Translation (NAT)
An application that translates the IP address of the sending host to another IP address while relaying the TCP/IP data to another network.

Class B Addresses

Class B addresses have first octets with a decimal number between 128 and 191. For example:

128.*x*.*y*.*z*

151.*x*.*y*.*z*

165.*x*.*y*.*z*

191.*x*.*y*.*z*

In binary, a Class B address always starts with 10 as the two leftmost bits. For example:

128.*x*.*y*.*z* =	1000 0000.*x*.*y*.*z*
151.*x*.*y*.*z* =	1001 0111.*x*.*y*.*z*
165.*x*.*y*.*z* =	1010 0101.*x*.*y*.*z*
191.*x*.*y*.*z* =	1011 1111.*x*.*y*.*z*

Notice that 191 has a 1 in every bit of the octet except the second leftmost bit. The next higher binary value will put a 1 in the second leftmost bit, and the resulting address will not be a Class B. Therefore, 191.*x.y.z* is the highest Class B address.

Class B addresses use the first two octets to represent the unique network address and leave only two octets to develop unique host addresses on that network. Because there is a 10 in the first two bits, the following six bits in the first octet and all eight bits in the second octet are used to distinguish this network from all other networks. Sixteen bits are used by each host to make itself unique on the network. The equation that proves the number of Class B networks is:

$$2^{14} = 16{,}384$$

This means that there are 16,384 Class B networks available. On each of these 16,384 networks, each address uses the other 16 bits to make itself unique. All possible combinations of these 16 bits make up the number of unique host IP addresses that can be on each of those 16,384 networks. There are 65,534 possible unique IP addresses on each of the 16,384 Class B networks:

$$2^{16} - 2 = 65{,}534$$

Class C Addresses

The Class C addresses have first octets with a decimal number between 192 and 223. For example:

192.*x.y.z*

200.*x.y.z*

210.*x.y.z*

223.*x.y.z*

In binary, a Class C address always starts with 110 as the three leftmost bits. For example:

192.*x.y.z* =   11000000.*x.y.z*

200.*x.y.z* =   11001000.*x.y.z*

210.*x.y.z* =   11010010.*x.y.z*

223.*x.y.z* =   1101 1111.*x.y.z*

Notice that 223 has a 1 in every bit of the octet except the third leftmost bit. The next higher binary value will put a 1 in the third leftmost bit, and the resulting address will not be a Class C. Therefore, 223.*x.y.z* is the highest Class C address.

Class C addresses use the first three octets to represent the unique network address and leave only one octet to develop unique host addresses on that network. Because the first three bits in the first octet are 110, the network portion of a Class C address includes the remaining five bits in the first octet, all eight bits in the second octet, and all eight bits in the third octet, for a total of 21 bits. That leaves only eight bits to be used by each host to make itself unique on this network.

The equation for Class C networks is:

$$2^{21} = 2{,}097{,}152$$

This means that there are 2,097,152 Class C networks available. On each of these 2,097,152 networks, each address uses the other eight bits to make itself unique. All possible combinations of these eight bits make up the number of unique host IP addresses that can be on each of those 2,097,152 networks. There are 254 possible unique IP addresses on each of the 2,097,152 Class C networks:

$$2^{8} - 2 = 254$$

Class D Addresses

Class D addresses have decimal values between 224 and 239 in the first octet. In the first octet, the first four bits are 1110.

Class A, B, and C are the only address classes that are available for TCP/IP host IP addresses. In contrast, no one host can have a Class D address. These addresses are called **multicast** addresses, and they are invalid for any workstation or host to use.

The purpose of a multicast address is to enable a server somewhere to send data to a Class D address that no one host has so that several hosts can listen to that address at the same time. When you are watching TV on the Internet or listening to the radio on the Internet, your computer is listening to a Class D address. No server is sending data directly to your workstation; instead, a server is sending data to the multicast address. Any host can use software to listen for data at that address, and many hosts can be listening at once.

Class E Addresses

The last class of addresses is Class E. Class E addresses range from 240–255 in the first octet, and the four leftmost bits are 1111.

Class E addresses are reserved addresses and are invalid host addresses. They are used for experimental purposes by the IETF.

Classless Inter-Domain Routing (CIDR)

Classless Inter-Domain Routing (CIDR) is an IP addressing scheme that was developed after the class system of A, B, C, D, and E. The traditional class system considers an IP address as four octets with the network portion of the address highlighted by a subnet mask. The standard network portion is the first octet, the first two octets, or the first three octets. CIDR addressing still represents IP addresses in the traditional dotted decimal notation, but highlights the network portion with a slash followed by a number. For example:

```
192.168.3.15/26
172.21.165.1/19
```

The number after the slash is the number of bits that represent the network portion of the IP address. CIDR was developed to increase the efficiency of address allocation and to alleviate overloaded Internet routers. Using CIDR addressing, fewer and shorter addresses/routes need to be entered into the routing tables.

---

multicast

A communication between a single sender and multiple receivers on a network. No one host can have this address, but several can receive data by listening to it.

Classless Inter-Domain Routing (CIDR)

An IP addressing scheme that uses a slash followed by a number to highlight the network portion of an address instead of using a subnet mask.

IP Address Class Summary

It is important to understand the overall scheme of addresses. Then, as you make decisions about the TCP/IP addressing scheme for your network, you will use a network address that enables you to address all the hosts on the network and that allows room for growth.

To summarize the rules and equations for Class A, B, and C addressing:

◆ A host ID cannot be all 0s.

◆ A host ID cannot be all 1s.

◆ To determine the number of networks that can be created, use the formula 2^N where N is the number of bits in the network portion of the address.

◆ To determine the number of hosts that can be created, use the formula $2^N - 2$ where N is the number of bits in the host portion of the address.

Following is a chart summarizing the classes of addresses:

Class	Range	Leftmost Bits	# of Network Bits	# of Networks	# of Host Bits	# of Hosts
A	1–127	0	8	126	24	16,777,214
B	128–191	10	16	16,384	16	65,534
C	192–223	110	24	2,097,152	8	254
D	224–239	1110	INVALID			
E	240–255	1111	INVALID			

Review Questions

1. Convert the following binary numbers to their decimal equivalents:
   a. 1100 0011
   b. 1010 0101
   c. 1001 1011
   d. 1110 0111

   _____

   _____

   _____

   _____

2. Convert the following decimal numbers to their binary equivalents:
   a. 10
   b. 57
   c. 127
   d. 255

   _____

   _____

   _____

   _____

3. What is the range of first octet addresses for the following classes?
   a. Class A
   b. Class B
   c. Class C

   _____

   _____

   _____

4. What is a Class D address used for?

_____

5. How many hosts can be on a Class C network?

_____

6. How many Class B networks are there?

_____

7. How many hosts can be on a Class A network?

_____

8. What does a host address with all 1s represent?

_____

9. What does a host address with all 0s represent?

_____

10. When is a host address of all 0s or all 1s invalid?

_____

11. What is the equation used to find the number of hosts that a network can have?

_____

Chapter

7

Addressing
IP Hosts

In this chapter, you are going to look at the different ways of assigning IP addresses to each host. There are two methods of assigning IP addresses: manual configuration and automatic configuration. Most of this chapter focuses on the second method, which uses the Dynamic Host Control Protocol.

In this chapter, you will learn about:

 Installing TCP/IP

 Assigning IP addresses

 Obtaining an IP address from a DHCP server

 Renewing IP addresses

 Reserving IP addresses

 Setting the Lease Duration

 Setting DHCP scopes and options

Installing and Assigning IP Addresses

Because every host has to have a unique IP address, somebody needs to assign an IP address to each host. Other optional pieces of configuration information might also need to be assigned to a host, such as a default gateway, a Domain Name System (DNS) server, a Windows Internet Naming Service (WINS) server, and many other options.

Two methods are used to assign IP addresses: manual configuration and automatic configuration. Both are discussed in later in this section.

There are several operating systems and procedures for installing and configuring an IP address. The following instructions and screen captures will guide you through installing TCP/IP in two of the most popular operating systems: Windows NT and Windows 95/98.

Installing TCP/IP on Windows NT

To install TCP/IP on Windows NT, follow these steps:

1. Access the Network settings by clicking Start ➤ Settings ➤ Control Panel and then double-clicking Network. Or, on the Windows NT desktop, right-click Network Neighborhood and then click Properties. The following dialog box appears.

2. Begin adding the TCP/IP protocol by clicking the Protocols tab and then clicking the Add button.

3. In the Select Network Protocol dialog box that appears next, choose the TCP/IP protocol by clicking that option. Then click OK, as shown below.

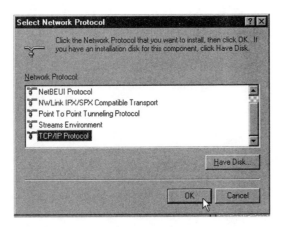

4. In the TCP/IP Setup dialog, choose to use DHCP or to manually assign an IP address by clicking Yes or No. If you choose Yes, you are prompted later to fill in all TCP/IP information. If you choose No, a DHCP server will supply all TCP/IP configuration information.

5. In the Windows NT Setup dialog shown below, supply a path to the Windows NT system files. System files are needed to complete the protocol installation. Depending on your installation, the system files may already be on the hard drive, or you may need the NT installation CD. Click the Continue button.

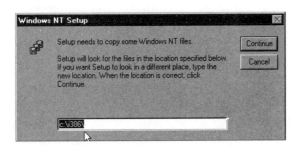

6. Several files are copied, and the installation stops at the Network Settings page. Click the Close button. More files are copied, and then you are prompted to type the IP address information if you chose No in step 4. Reboot if you are prompted to.

Installing TCP/IP on Windows 95/98

To install TCP/IP for Windows 95/98, take the following steps:

1. Access the Network settings by clicking Start ➢ Settings ➢ Control Panel and double-clicking Network. Or, on the Windows 95/98 desktop, right-click Network Neighborhood and then click Properties. The following dialog box appears.

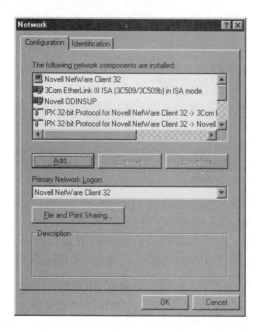

2. Begin adding the TCP/IP protocol by ensuring that you are on the Configuration page and then clicking the Add button.

3. In the Select Network Type dialog box shown below, select the Protocol option as the type of network component to install. Then, click the Add button.

4. On the Select Network Protocol page, select the TCP/IP protocol: On the Manufacturers side of the screen, click Microsoft and on the Network Protocols side of the screen, click TCP/IP. Then, click OK.

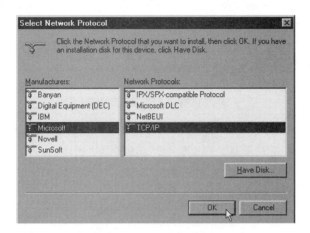

5. To complete the installation, click OK and then reboot.

NOTE

Windows 95/98 is installed set to use DHCP. After rebooting, you can modify the configuration if desired.

Manual IP Address Configuration

An administrator with only a few hosts on a network may determine that the best method of assigning IP addresses is to do so manually. An administrator who has 10 hosts on a network, for example, might sit in front of each of the 10 hosts and input the IP address, subnet mask, and possibly some other optional addresses. This may be the preferred method because there are only a few hosts to address.

However, an administrator with 254 hosts on a network would have to type in all the information at each of the 254 hosts. While inputting this information 254 times, chances are the administrator would make a couple of typos here and there. Those typos might be difficult to troubleshoot. An administrator with 2,540 hosts would have a lot more typing to do and probably would make a lot more typos and face a lot of extra troubleshooting.

Therefore, manually configuring IP addresses is usually done for only a few hosts. Instead, most administrators choose to use Dynamic Host Configuration Protocol (DHCP) to assign IP addresses to the majority of their hosts. (See the later section on DHCP.)

Manually Assigning an IP Address for Windows NT

To manually assign an IP address for Windows NT, take the following steps:

1. Access the Network settings by clicking Start ➢ Settings ➢ Control Panel and then double-clicking Network. Or, on the Windows NT desktop, right-click Network Neighborhood and then click Properties. The following dialog box appears.

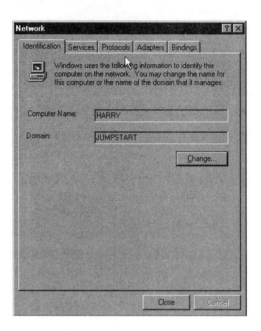

2. Access the TCP/IP properties by clicking the Protocols tab, the TCP/IP option, and then the Properties button, as shown below.

3. You are now viewing the Microsoft TCP/IP Properties dialog box shown below. This is where you can choose to either put in the address manually or obtain an address from a DHCP server. Choose to enter the IP address manually by clicking the radio button labeled Specify an IP Address.

4. Enter the configuration information: the IP address, the subnet mask, and the default gateway. The default subnet mask will appear after the IP address is supplied; you must overwrite it if you want to modify it. Although the default gateway is an optional parameter, it is usually configured. You need to specify a default gateway if this host will be sending data to a host on another network.

5. Save the configuration by clicking OK on the TCP/IP Properties page and then clicking OK on the Network Protocols page. Reboot if prompted.

Manually Assigning an IP Address for Windows 95/98

To manually assign an IP address for Windows 95/98, take the following steps:

1. Access the Network settings by clicking Start ➤ Settings ➤ Control Panel and then double-clicking Network. Or, on the Windows 95/98 desktop, right-click Network Neighborhood and click Properties.

2. Access the TCP/IP properties by clicking the Configuration tab. Then scroll to TCP/IP and click that option. Finally, click the Properties button. If there is more than one TCP/IP line, choose the one that corresponds to the name of the network card in the computer.

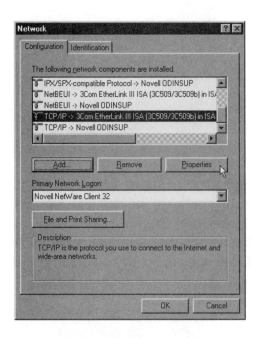

3. You are now viewing the TCP/IP Properties dialog box. This is where you can choose to either enter the address manually or obtain an address from a DHCP server. Click the radio button labeled Specify an IP Address to enter the IP address manually.

4. Enter the configuration information: the IP address and the subnet mask.

5. Configure the default gateway by clicking the Gateway tab, typing in the default gateway, and clicking the Add button. Although the default gateway is an optional parameter, it is usually configured. You need to specify a default gateway if this host will be sending data to a host on another network. Click OK on the Gateway page and again on the Configuration page, and reboot if prompted.

DHCP server

A host running a service to lease IP addresses to other hosts. The DHCP server is configured by an administrator with the pool, or scope, of addresses to be leased.

---

scope

A pool of IP addresses that a DHCP server leases to DHCP clients.

Dynamic Host Control Protocol (DHCP)

DHCP is the automatic IP-address giver. In essence, an administrator configures a **DHCP server** with a pool of addresses to lease out to hosts. The administrator may configure the server to lease out addresses to different networks by creating several pools of addresses.

Each pool of addresses contains the information that a TCP/IP host needs to build a TCP/IP stack. The pool is sometimes referred to as a **scope**, or range, of addresses. As a DHCP client is building its TCP/IP stack, it requests an IP address, and the DHCP server looks in the pools of addresses to see whether there are any IP addresses that can be leased out to the network that the host is on.

The client doesn't already have an IP address because the administrator did not type one in. Instead, the administrator determined that the client should get its IP address automatically from a DHCP server. So the client broadcasts a packet out onto the network; the packet says something like, "Hey! Who's the DHCP server?"

After a DHCP server receives a packet indicating that a DHCP client is looking for a DHCP server, the server examines its pools of addresses and possibly offers an IP address to the client. If the DHCP server is not configured with a pool of addresses for the network where the DHCP client is located, the request is ignored.

The DHCP client might receive offers from several DHCP servers. The client selects the first one that it receives and sends back a packet that says, "Yeah, I would like that IP address." That packet goes back to the DHCP server, and the DHCP server responds with a packet that says, "All right, you can have that IP address."

In the following sections, you will examine the four-step process that a DHCP client goes through to obtain an IP address from a DHCP server.

The DHCP Process

The four-step process of DHCP can easily be remembered by using the mnemonic of DORA:

- ◇ Discover
- ◇ Offer
- ◇ Request
- ◇ Acknowledgment

Obtaining an IP Address from a DHCP Server

DHCP discover

The first step in using DHCP to lease an IP address. A DHCP discover packet is broadcast saying, "Hey, who is a DHCP server?"

There are four steps in getting an IP address from a DHCP server: DHCP discover, DHCP offer, DHCP request, and DHCP acknowledgement.

Let's walk through these steps and examine the packets at each.

DHCP Discover

The first step is the broadcast of a **DHCP discover** packet. As the client is building its TCP/IP stack, it broadcasts a message that says, "Hey! I need a DHCP server!" The client broadcasts this packet so that no configuration is necessary. No administrator needs to type in the address of the DHCP server. Also, the client that is looking for a DHCP server has to broadcast the discover packet so that all hosts on the network will receive it—one of which is hopefully a DHCP server.

In the illustration below, Harry the Host represents a DHCP client. The first thing that Harry needs to do is find a DHCP server. Because Harry doesn't know where one is, nor does he have an address yet, he broadcasts a DHCP discover packet to help find one.

The following screen capture shows the Ethernet portion of the DHCP request packet. The Ethernet destination address is FFFFFFFFFFFF because that is the broadcast hardware address. The Ethernet source address is 005004818D42, which is the hardware address of the DHCP client.

```
Frame Src MAC Addr Dst MAC Addr  Protocol Description                                       S
3     HARRY        *BROADCAST    DHCP     Request          (xid=5F444C10)                  0 ▲
4     DHCP-SERVER  *BROADCAST    DHCP     ACK              (xid=5F444C10)                  D:
◄                                                                                          ► ▼

♣FRAME: Base frame properties                                                                ▲
━ETHERNET: ETYPE = 0x0800 : Protocol = IP:  DOD Internet Protocol
 ♣ETHERNET: Destination address : FFFFFFFFFFFF
 ♣ETHERNET: Source address : 005004818D42      ☐
  ETHERNET: Frame Length : 342 (0x0156)
  ETHERNET: Ethernet Type : 0x0800 (IP:  DOD Internet Protocol)
  ETHERNET: Ethernet Data: Number of data bytes remaining = 328 (0x0148)
♣IP: ID = 0xF500; Proto = UDP; Len: 328
♣UDP: IP Multicast:  Src Port: BOOTP Client, (68); Dst Port: BOOTP Server (67); Length = 308 (0x134)
♣DHCP: Request            (xid=5F444C10)
```

The following screen capture shows the remainder of the DHCP request packet. In the DHCP portion of the packet, the client's Ethernet address is listed again. In the DHCP Option Field, the DHCP requested address is listed, which in this packet is 192.168.2.171. The DHCP server's address is also listed, which is 192.168.2.254. As the packet is broadcast, the DHCP server with the address 192.168.2.254 will know that the DHCP client is requesting the offered IP address. All other DHCP servers that had offered an IP address to the client with the hardware address of 005004818D42 will put the IP address offered back into the pool of available addresses.

```
Frame Src MAC Addr Dst MAC Addr  Protocol Description                                       S
3     HARRY        *BROADCAST    DHCP     Request          (xid=5F444C10)                  0 ▲
4     DHCP-SERVER  *BROADCAST    DHCP     ACK              (xid=5F444C10)                  D:
◄                                                                                          ► ▼

♣IP: ID = 0xF500; Proto = UDP; Len: 328                                                      ▲
♣UDP: IP Multicast:  Src Port: BOOTP Client, (68); Dst Port: BOOTP Server (67); Length = 308 (0x134)
━DHCP: Request            (xid=5F444C10)
  DHCP: Op Code          (op)     = 1 (0x1)
  DHCP: Hardware Type    (htype)  = 1 (0x1) 10Mb Ethernet
  DHCP: Hardware Address Length (hlen) = 6 (0x6)
  DHCP: Hops             (hops)   = 0 (0x0)
  DHCP: Transaction ID   (xid)    = 1598311440 (0x5F444C10)
  DHCP: Seconds          (secs)   = 0 (0x0)
 ♣DHCP: Flags            (flags)  = 0 (0x0)
  DHCP: Client IP Address (ciaddr) = 0.0.0.0
  DHCP: Your   IP Address (yiaddr) = 0.0.0.0
  DHCP: Server IP Address (siaddr) = 0.0.0.0
  DHCP: Relay  IP Address (giaddr) = 0.0.0.0
  DHCP: Client Ethernet Address (chaddr) = 005004818D42
  DHCP: Server Host Name  (sname) = <Blank>
  DHCP: Boot File Name    (file)  = <Blank>
  DHCP: Magic Cookie = [OK]
━DHCP: Option Field       (options)
  DHCP: DHCP Message Type     = DHCP Request
  DHCP: Client-identifier     = (Type: 1) 00 50 04 81 8d 42
  DHCP: Requested Address     = 192.168.2.171
  DHCP: Server Identifier     = 192.168.2.254
  DHCP: Host Name             = HARRY
  DHCP: Parameter Request List = (Length: 7) 01 0f 03 2c 2e 2f 06
  DHCP: End of this option field                                                             ▼
```

DHCP Acknowledgment

Now the deal is almost done. A DHCP client was looking for a DHCP server to lease an IP address from, and a DHCP server heard the discover packet and sent an offer. The offer was received, and a request to use that address was made. Now all that needs to be done is to sign the lease papers and the deal is closed.

The DHCP server receives the DHCP request and prepares a packet to close the deal. This packet is called a **DHCP acknowledgment (ack)** packet. Like the other packets, this one is also broadcast because the DHCP client still does not have a valid IP address. The DHCP ack packet simply says, "I received your request for the IP address that I offered you, and yes, you can have that address. By the way, here are all the options that come with that address."

The following illustration shows the final packet in the DHCP sequence. Donna broadcasts a DCHP ack, which is the acknowledgement packet. After Harry receives this, he knows that the deal is done and he has a valid lease on his new IP address.

DHCP acknowledgment (ack)

The final step in using DHCP to lease a new IP address or to renew an IP address lease. A DHCP ack is broadcast for new IP address leases and sent directly to the DHCP client for renewals. The packet says, "It's a done deal! You can have this IP address, and here are some extra parameters that you can have."

The next screen capture shows the Ethernet portion of the DHCP ack packet. The Ethernet destination address is FFFFFFFFFFFF, which is the broadcast hardware address, and the Ethernet source address is 005004744FFF, which is the hardware address of the DHCP server.

The DHCP portion of the DHCP ack packet contains information about the IP address and the lease parameters. The following screen capture shows the DHCP portion with all the DHCP options. After the DHCP client receives this acknowledgment, then the client has an IP address. Now that the client has a valid lease on an IP address, the client finishes building its TCP/IP stack.

DHCP Leases

Because IP addresses are leased from the DHCP server, the DHCP client must renew the lease on the address at a specified time. If the lease were to expire, the host would cease to be able to communicate using TCP/IP.

Time To Live (TTL)
The amount of time that the lease on an IP address is valid.

When half of the **Time To Live (TTL)** value has expired, the DHCP client will send a DHCP request to the DHCP server asking for a new lease. For example, if the IP address is leased for 24 hours, after 12 hours the DHCP client will send a DHCP request directly to the DHCP server. The DHCP request is not broadcast this time because the DHCP client has a valid IP address and a valid lease, and the client knows the IP address of the DHCP server. Notice in the previous DHCP acknowledgment packet that an option field specifies an IP address lease time. This is the way that the DHCP server informs the client of the length of the lease. The length of lease was also specified in the offer packet.

In the next screen capture, a DHCP client is sending a DHCP request to renew the lease on an IP address. In the Ethernet portion of the DHCP request packet, both the Ethernet destination and source addresses are filled in with the appropriate hardware addresses. This is not a broadcast. In the IP portion of the DHCP request, the IP addresses of the client and of the server are filled in. Including the server's IP address enables the packet to be routed to the correct network (and therefore the DHCP client does not have to broadcast the request).

```
Frame Src MAC Addr  Dst MAC Addr  Protocol Description                                 S
1     HARRY         DHCP-SERVER   DHCP     Request        (xid=37D473CF)              1
2     DHCP-SERVER   HARRY         DHCP     ACK            (xid=37D473CF)              D

FRAME: Base frame properties
ETHERNET: ETYPE = 0x0800 : Protocol = IP:  DOD Internet Protocol
  ETHERNET: Destination address : 005004744FFF
  ETHERNET: Source address : 005004818D42
  ETHERNET: Frame Length : 342 (0x0156)
  ETHERNET: Ethernet Type : 0x0800 (IP:  DOD Internet Protocol)
  ETHERNET: Ethernet Data: Number of data bytes remaining = 328 (0x0148)
IP: ID = 0xD000; Proto = UDP; Len: 328
  IP: Version = 4 (0x4)
  IP: Header Length = 20 (0x14)
  IP: Service Type = 0 (0x0)
  IP: Total Length = 328 (0x148)
  IP: Identification = 53248 (0xD000)
  IP: Flags Summary = 0 (0x0)
  IP: Fragment Offset = 0 (0x0) bytes
  IP: Time to Live = 128 (0x80)
  IP: Protocol = UDP - User Datagram
  IP: Checksum = 0xE2AA
  IP: Source Address = 192.168.2.171
  IP: Destination Address = 192.168.2.254
  IP: Data: Number of data bytes remaining = 308 (0x0134)
UDP: Src Port: BOOTP Client, (68); Dst Port: BOOTP Server (67); Length = 308 (0x134)
DHCP: Request            (xid=37D473CF)
```

118

The DHCP server receives the DHCP request and sends back a DHCP ack. This packet is sent directly to the client requesting the IP address. The DHCP ack includes all the options and a new TTL. The following screen capture shows the DHCP ack with the DHCP parameters that are being sent back to the client.

The process of renewing the IP address lease after only half of the TTL keeps the DHCP clients coming back often, and well before the expiration time. If there are any problems renewing the address, plenty of time remains to rectify them. For example, if the DHCP client sends a DHCP request after half of the TTL and the DHCP server does not respond, it is not yet a problem because the client still has a valid lease.

If ⅞ of the TTL has expired, and the client has not successfully renewed the lease, the DHCP client will broadcast a DHCP request so that any DHCP server can respond with a DHCP ack. A DHCP server may also respond with a DHCP nack (negative acknowledgment). A DHCP nack says that the client cannot use that IP address any longer. If the DHCP client receives a DHCP nack or the TTL expires, the client will cease using any TCP/IP communication. If the user is working with locally installed applications and is not using any networked applications, the user can continue working. If the user is using networked applications when the lease expires, those applications will terminate.

DHCP IP Address Renewal

When a DHCP client is restarted and still has a valid lease on its IP address, a DHCP request containing the leased IP address is broadcast onto the network. The DHCP server sends a DHCP ack to the client, which renews the lease on the IP address. If the DHCP client does not get a DHCP ack and the TTL has not expired, the client will continue to use the IP address. Another DHCP server on the network may send a DHCP nack, which will cause the DHCP client to cease using that IP address and start all over again by broadcasting a DHCP discover packet.

When a DHCP client shuts down, it does not release the IP address that it has leased. There are times when an administrator would like a DHCP client to release the IP address back to the DHCP server, however. This may be because the administrator is troubleshooting or because the DHCP client will not need an IP address anymore, for example, when it's leaving the network. Most implementations of the DHCP client software allow the user to release the IP address at any time.

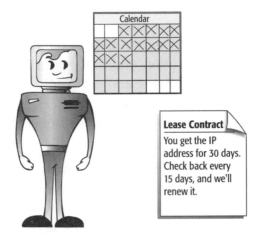

Reserving DHCP IP Addresses

A DHCP server randomly assigns IP addresses to clients on the network. But a network administrator might prefer some hosts to always have the same IP addresses. These hosts can use a manually assigned IP address. A manual configuration requires the administrator either to type in the IP address configuration information or to make a reservation.

An IP address reservation is set at the DHCP server. The administrator sets up a reservation for the host by entering the host's hardware address and the IP address into a reservation list. Whenever a DHCP request is received, the DHCP server sees the hardware address and matches it to the IP address that has been reserved for it. The DHCP offer that is sent back out will include the reserved IP address.

Some examples of hosts that an administrator will want to always have the same IP addresses are:

Servers   Applications may be mapped to use a particular IP address.

Printers   Hosts may be configured to print to a printer with a particular address.

Routers   Hosts are configured with an address for their router (default gateway).

An administrator might also need to reserve IP addresses when the number of addresses for a network is limited. If an administrator has 254 valid IP addresses and 300 hosts on the network, there could be a problem: If all hosts need an IP address at the same time, some will fail to get one and therefore will not be able to communicate on the network. Probably not all the hosts will be turned on and using an IP address at the same time. So, chances are that this scheme will work fine, but the administrator will want to make sure that the CEO always gets an IP address. To do so, the administrator should get the hardware address of the CEO's workstation and reserve one IP address on the DHCP server for the CEO's computer. Then the CEO is always guaranteed an IP address. The administrator had better be sure to type in the hardware address correctly or the CEO will never get the IP address that has been reserved.

Setting the Lease Duration

Setting the length of the TTL is up to the administrator. A long TTL means that the DHCP clients will not have to renew their IP addresses for a long time. It also means that the IP addresses will not be available to any other host for a long time.

Let's say that a user from our New York office is visiting the San Diego office and has a DHCP-enabled laptop. When the user plugs into the network in San Diego, the laptop broadcasts a DHCP discover. A DHCP server responds and a lease is consummated with the laptop. If the lease is for 30 days, the DHCP server will not lease that address to any other DHCP client for that time period.

If the laptop leaves the San Diego network later that same day, the DHCP server does not know that the laptop has left and doesn't need the IP address anymore. The IP address is gone for 30 days even though it is not being used; the DHCP server will not return it to the available pool of addresses until the lease has expired. Meanwhile, the DHCP clients on the San Diego network have one less IP address to use.

If the administrator had set the TTL to 24 hours, the IP address would be available the next day to be leased to another DHCP client. However, every 12 hours all the DHCP clients would be renewing their leases. This would cause some added network traffic that might be unnecessary.

Many Internet Service Providers (ISPs) use DHCP with a short TTL. A TTL of two hours will cause the DHCP clients to renew their lease every hour, but IP addresses are returned to the available pool more frequently. Therefore, the ISP can have fewer IP addresses than clients because they will not all be in use at the same time and are reused within two hours.

When IP addresses are at a premium and there aren't many available in the pool, an administrator should set a short TTL. This way, leases are expiring sooner, and the DHCP server will have the address back sooner to re-lease. An administrator should also set a short lease when the options are undergoing frequent changes (for example, when the address of the DNS server, WINS server, or default gateway is going to change). A shorter TTL requires the DHCP clients to renew their leases more often, and their associated options can be updated then. However, if the pool is rich with addresses and a tremendous amount of unused addresses are in the pool, an administrator can set the TTL for much longer.

Setting DHCP Scopes and Options

An administrator must configure the DHCP server with the appropriate scopes, or pools, of addresses and DHCP options. After the server is set up correctly, DHCP clients will begin getting IP addresses, and no further setup is required.

As stated earlier in this chapter, the range of IP addresses is referred to as a scope of addresses. Besides the IP address, the scope includes the subnet mask, a TTL, and possibly other options such as a default gateway. As DHCP discover packets are received, the DHCP server randomly offers IP addresses starting from the lower end of the scope.

The administrator needs to enter the scope options. The options include any addressing information that should be included with the IP address. Some common options included with an address from a DHCP server are:

- ✧ IP address of one or more DNS servers
- ✧ IP address of the WINS server
- ✧ IP address of the default gateway

If the administrator has manually assigned an IP address, it must be excluded from the scope of addresses. For example, if the administrator has manually configured a server with the IP address of 192.168.2.5, it is important that the DHCP server not offer that address to any DHCP clients. If the DHCP server has been set up to offer addresses in the range of 192.168.2.1 through 192.168.2.150, then the administrator must make an **exclusion** for the address 192.168.2.5.

A DHCP option that is set for all scopes that a DHCP server services is called a **global option**. A DHCP option that is set for just one scope is called a **scope option**. If any options are set for just one particular address, that is done as part of the reservation for that IP address.

One of the benefits of DHCP is that the DHCP clients come back to renew the leases on their addresses. If any option needs to be changed, an administrator has to change it only at the server, and when the DHCP clients come back to renew their leases, all the new options get sent out with the DHCP ack. The administrator has to manually update those options at the hosts if their IP address was manually configured.

exclusion
An IP address that falls into a range of addresses to be leased, but that has been set by an administrator not to be leased.

global option
A parameter that is set at the DHCP server and that applies to all scopes of IP addresses that this DHCP server serves.

scope option
A parameter that is set at the DHCP server that applies to only one scope of IP addresses.

Review Questions

Terms to Know
- ❏ DHCP server
- ❏ scope
- ❏ DHCP discover
- ❏ DHCP offer
- ❏ DHCP request
- ❏ DHCP ack
- ❏ TTL
- ❏ exclusion
- ❏ global option
- ❏ scope option

1. What are two ways to assign IP addresses to hosts?

   _____

   _____

2. What are the four steps of using DHCP?

   _____

   _____

   _____

   _____

3. Which of the four steps uses a broadcast packet?

   _____

4. What information is included in a discover packet?

   _____

5. What information is included in an offer packet?

   _____

6. Why would an administrator use a reservation?

   _____

7. When should an administrator use DHCP instead of manually configuring IP addresses?

   _____

8. When does a DHCP client renew the lease of an address?

_____

9. When a DHCP offer is sent onto the network, how does the client know which host the packet is intended for?

_____

10. List some hosts for which a network administrator should consider using manually assigned IP addresses.

_____

_____

_____

Chapter
8

Subnet Masks

Subnet masks are one of the most interesting aspects of TCP/IP. Subnet masks point out to IP which bits of the 32-bit IP address refer to the network. A good network administrator understands how to determine and use subnet masks. In this chapter, you will examine the following topics:

 Standard subnet masks

 Custom subnet masks

 How to create custom subnet masks

What Is a Subnet Mask?

A **subnet mask** is a number that looks like an IP address. It shows TCP/IP how many bits are used for the network portion of the IP address by covering up, or "masking," the IP address's network portion.

Just as people use an area code to determine whether a telephone number is local or long distance, TCP/IP uses the subnet mask to determine whether another host is local or remote.

Every IP address must have a subnet mask.

As you learned in Chapter 6, an IP address is made up of two parts: the network portion and the host portion. For every outgoing packet, IP has to determine whether the destination host is on the same **local network** or on a **remote network**. If the destination is local, then IP can use an ARP broadcast to get the hardware address of the destination host. If the destination is not on the local network, an ARP broadcast would get stopped by a router.

Therefore, IP sends packets that are bound for a remote network directly to the router, also known as the default gateway. The router then sends the packet to the next network, on a journey to the correct destination network. To send the packet directly to the router, IP first sends an ARP broadcast to get the router's hardware address.

Below, Harry the Host is sending data to Amber, another host on a different network. TCP/IP uses the subnet mask to simply determine whether a destination IP address is on the local network or on a remote network.

subnet mask
A 32-bit address that looks like an IP address but actually points out to IP which part of the IP address is the network portion.

local network
Hosts that are on the same side of a router are considered on the same local network. Two hosts on the same local network have the exact same bit values in the network portion of their IP addresses.

remote network
Hosts that have a router separating them are considered on a remote network from each other. Two hosts on remote networks have different bit values in the network portion of their IP addresses.

Network and Host

Applying a subnet mask is like looking through a set of "**subnet goggles.**" Imagine wearing a set of goggles as you look at an IP address; you see all 32 bits, each in their own slot. When you ask the question, "How many bits are used for the network portion of this IP address?" the subnet mask lights up the slots that are in the network portion of the address.

Through subnet goggles, 255.0.0.0 look like this:

    NNNN NNNN.HHHH HHHH.HHHH HHHH.HHHH HHHH

The goggles light up the first eight bits as the network portion (**N**), and the remaining 24 bits are used for the host portion (H).

Through subnet goggles, 255.255.0.0 look like this:

    NNNN NNNN.NNNN NNNN.HHHH HHHH.HHHH HHHH

The goggles light up the first 16 bits as the network portion.

The subnet mask simply provides a means to light up the correct slots so that IP can figure out the number of bits used for the network portion of the address. After IP figures this out, IP can compare the address to that of another host to determine whether that host is local or remote.

subnet goggles
A fictional set of goggles that IP wears when looking at an IP address to determine whether an address is local or remote. The goggles "light up" the network and subnet bits with 1s as the bit values in the subnet mask.

Identifying a Local or Remote Network

With every packet that is sent across a network, the big question is: Is the destination address local or remote? The destination is local if the network portion of the source's IP address is the same as that of the destination's IP address.

If any bit of the network portions differ from each other, then the destination is remote. This is similar to figuring out whether someone lives on the same street as you do. Look at the person's street name; if it is the same as yours, the person lives on the same street that you do. If any part of the street name is different, the person is remote to your street.

But, as stated earlier, before IP can figure out whether the destination address is remote, IP has to determine how many bits are in the network portion of the source IP address. IP uses the subnet mask to determine which bits of the IP address represent the network portion of the address.

The subnet mask is 32 bits long, but people use **dotted decimal notation** to represent it, just as they do with an IP address. A subnet mask, in binary, is made up of several contiguous 1s, which represent the network portion of the address, and then the rest of the bits are 0s. When determining how many of the 32 bits are in the network portion of an IP address, IP looks at the subnet mask for the contiguous 1s.

For example, if the first 16 bits are set to 1, then IP compares the first 16 bits of the source IP address with the first 16 bits of the destination IP address. If these 16 bits are exactly the same, the destination host is local; if any of the bits are different, the destination host is remote. If the first 24 bits are set to 1, then IP compares the first 24 bits of the source IP address with the first 24 bits of the destination IP address. If these 24 bits are exactly the same, the destination host is local; if any of the bits are different, the destination host is remote.

Finding a Local Address

A subnet mask of 255.0.0.0 in decimal converts to this binary number:

```
1111 1111.0000 0000.0000 0000.0000 0000
```

This binary number tells IP that the first eight bits are used in the network portion of the address, and the last 24 bits are used in the host portion of the address.

For example, if the source IP address is 10.1.2.3 with a subnet mask of 255.0.0.0, and the destination address is 10.3.4.5, then IP examines the addresses like this:

	Decimal	Binary
Subnet Mask	255.0.0.0	1111 1111.0000 0000.0000 0000.0000 0000
Source	10.1.2.3	0000 1010.0000 0001.0000 0010.0000 0011
Destination	10.3.4.5	0000 1010.0000 0011.0000 0100.0000 0101
RESULT		Same = Local

Based on the subnet mask having the first eight bits set to 1, IP compares the first eight bits of the source to the first eight bits of the destination. In this case, the first eight bits of both addresses are exactly the same, so the destination is local. Knowing that the destination host has a local address, IP can broadcast an ARP to get the hardware address.

Finding a Remote Address

In another example, if the source IP address is 10.1.2.3 with a subnet mask of 255.0.0.0, and the destination address is 11.3.4.5, then IP examines the addresses like this:

	Decimal	Binary
Subnet Mask	255.0.0.0	1111 1111.0000 0000.0000 0000.0000 0000
Source	10.1.2.3	0000 1010.0000 0001.0000 0010.0000 0011
Destination	11.3.4.5	0000 1011.0000 0011.0000 0100.0000 0101
RESULT		Different = Remote

Based on the subnet mask having the first eight bits set to 1, IP compares the first eight bits of the source to the first eight bits of the destination. In this case, the first eight bits of both addresses are *not* the same, so the destination is remote. Knowing that the destination host has a remote address, IP cannot broadcast an ARP to get the hardware address because a router will stop the broadcast. Instead, IP broadcasts an ARP for the router, which is where IP must send the packet to move it off of the local network and on its way to the remote network.

Standard Subnet Masks

In Chapter 6, you looked at the five classes of IP addresses. For each class of address, there is a standard, or default, subnet mask. Each is discussed in the following sections.

**standard
subnet mask**
Also called a default subnet mask. For Class A = 255.0.0.0, for Class B = 255.255.0.0, and for Class C = 255.255.255.0.

Class A Addresses

The **standard subnet mask** for a Class A address is 255.0.0.0. This tells IP that the first eight bits are used for the network portion of the IP address, and the remaining 24 bits are used for the host portion. IP looks at the 32 bits and uses the subnet mask to mask out the network portion of the address:

    NNNN NNNN.HHHH HHHH.HHHH HHHH.HHHH HHHH

Because 24 bits are left for the host portion of the address, there are almost 17 million unique host IP addresses for each Class A network address.

Class B Addresses

A Class B address has a standard subnet mask of 255.255.0.0. This mask tells IP that the first 16 bits are used for the network portion of the address, and the remaining 16 bits are used for the host portion:

    NNNN NNNN.NNNN NNNN.HHHH HHHH.HHHH HHHH

The 16 bits that are used for the host portion of the address can uniquely address more than 16,000 hosts on each Class B network.

Class C Addresses

A Class C address has a standard subnet mask of 255.255.255.0, which masks out the first 24 bits as the network portion and leaves the remaining 8 bits for the host portion:

    NNNN NNNN.NNNN NNNN.NNNN NNNN.HHHH HHHH

The eight bits used for the host portion can uniquely address 254 hosts on each of the Class C networks.

In summary:

Class	Standard mask (decimal)	Standard mask (binary)
A	255.0.0.0	1111 1111.0000 0000.0000 0000.0000 0000
B	255.255.0.0	1111 1111.1111 1111.0000 0000.0000 0000
C	255.255.255.0	1111 1111.1111 1111.1111 1111.0000 0000

However, in most cases using the standard subnet mask is not the optimal solution for designing a TCP/IP addressing plan. Most implementations use a variation of the standard subnet mask called a custom subnet mask, which is explained in the following section.

The following screen capture shows a custom subnet mask being used. Because the IP address has 10 in the first octet, this is a class A address, and the standard subnet mask is 255.0.0.0. However, the administrator has defined a custom subnet mask of 255.255.255.240, which enables him to create more networks with fewer hosts on each network.

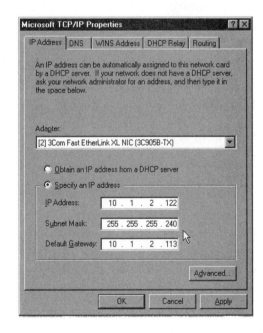

Custom Subnet Masks

On most networks, the network administrator uses an IP addressing scheme that includes a **custom subnet mask**. Because the routers that are in the physical local area network (LAN) define each network, a network administrator must use a different network address for each side of a router. When a router is used to create smaller networks, the smaller network is called a **subnet**.

A Class A address can have close to 17 million hosts on a network. However, no networks have 17 million hosts on one side of a router; it would not be physically possible. A large network is divided into several smaller networks by routers, and every time that a router is used, a new network address is required. Rather than obtain a new network address for each network, the network administrator can *create* more network addresses by using a custom subnet mask.

custom subnet mask

A non-standard subnet mask used by a network administrator to make more efficient use of a network address by creating more subnets.

subnet

A smaller network created by dividing a larger network.

A Custom Subnet Mask Analogy

Let's say that I win the lottery and suddenly have more money than I know what to do with. So the first thing I do is buy a huge new house. This enormous home has 50 bedrooms, 50 bathrooms, and 50 kitchens. This is a pretty big house for a family of four, so pretty soon we figure out that it is just too big. A better use of this house would be to subdivide it. I decide to put up a few walls and make 50 smaller homes, each with a bedroom, bathroom, and kitchen. To make the most efficient use of this huge home, I will have 50 families live in the apartments. This is a similar idea to subnetting an IP address.

The concept of a custom subnet mask is simple: Use the subnet mask to "take" some bits for the network portion of the IP address and use fewer bits for the host portion.

For example, a standard Class A subnet mask is 255.0.0.0, which uses eight bits to mask the network portion of the IP address. If an administrator is using a Class A address with this mask, then only eight bits can be used for the network portion of the address, and those eight bits are already set by which address is being used. In this scheme, 24 bits are left for the host portion, which means almost 17 million unique host addresses.

    255.0.0.0 =
    1111 1111.0000 0000.0000 0000.0000 0000

    NNNN NNNN.HHHH HHHH.HHHH HHHH.HHHH HHHH

A subnet mask of 255.255.0.0 masks 16 bits of the IP address for the network portion and leaves 16 bits for the host portion. If the administrator is using the same Class A address as before, but with a custom subnet mask of 255.255.0.0, then IP will use 16 bits as the network portion of the IP address. In this scheme, eight bits mask the Class A network address portion that was assigned as the network address. The first eight bits are the standard portion of the mask. The second eight bits mask the subnet portion (**S**), and 16 bits are still left for unique host addresses.

255.255.0.0 =
1111 1111.1111 1111.0000 0000.0000 0000
NNNN NNNN.*SSSS SSSS*.HHHH HHHH.HHHH HHHH

The following screen capture shows the display of the IP Subnet Calculator available from the Net3 Group, a company that conducts network analysis in the areas of consulting, training, and value-added software. The IP Subnet Calculator figures out the correct subnet mask, network addresses, and valid host IP addresses based on the parameters that you supply. Notice that the Class A is marked and eight subnet bits are requested. A standard Class A address uses the first eight bits and I am adding another eight bits in the subnet portion of the mask. The Decimal Network Mask in the bottom-left portion of the calculator shows the subnet mask is 255.255.0.0. In the center of the calculator, the bit map shows the significance of every bit in the subnet mask. The significance of each bit is displayed as either:

- ◆ n for network
- ◆ s for subnet
- ◆ h for host

Creating Additional Networks

With a custom subnet mask, the administrator still cannot change the first eight bits, which represent the assigned IP network address, but now can use the next eight bits to create more networks. This scheme still leaves 16 bits for the host portion of the address. Using the eight **subnet bits**, an administrator can create 254 subnets; and using the remaining 16 host bits, an administrator can address 65,534 hosts on each network.

To create the 254 subnets, simply use every binary variation of the eight subnet bits. For example:

Decimal	Binary
255.255.0.0	1111 1111.1111 1111.0000 0000.0000 0000
Subnet Goggles	NNNN NNNN.*SSSS SSSS*.HHHH HHHH.HHHH HHHH
10.1.0.0	0000 1010.*0000 0001*.HHHH HHHH.HHHH HHHH
10.2.0.0	0000 1010.*0000 0010*.HHHH HHHH.HHHH HHHH
10.3.0.0	0000 1010.*0000 0011*.HHHH HHHH.HHHH HHHH
10.4.0.0	0000 1010.*0000 0100*.HHHH HHHH.HHHH HHHH
10.5.0.0	0000 1010.*0000 0101*.HHHH HHHH.HHHH HHHH
10.6.0.0	0000 1010.*0000 0110*.HHHH HHHH.HHHH HHHH
10.7.0.0	0000 1010.*0000 0111*.HHHH HHHH.HHHH HHHH

Notice in the table above that the eight network (**N**) bits stay the same, and the eight subnet (**S**) bits are incrementing. This is how to create several unique networks. I've taken some bits from the host (H) portion of the address and given them to the network/subnet portion. In doing this, I am now able to create more networks that have fewer hosts on each of the networks. On each of these networks, 16 bits are still left for the host portion of the address, which can make up the 65,534 unique host addresses.

subnet bits

Bits used in the subnet mask to extend the number of bits available for the network portion of the IP address.

Subnetting Rules

If an administrator has a Class A address and needs to create more than 254 networks, then the appropriate subnet mask will extend to the next octet. An administrator needs to determine the number of networks to be addressed and the maximum number of hosts to be addressed on those networks, and then create the proper subnet mask. Sometimes the subnet mask will use an entire octet and sometimes it won't. An administrator can use any number of subnet bits to create the correct subnet mask.

broadcast
A packet that is intended to go to all hosts on a network. Routers will generally stop broadcasts from moving on to another network.

However, there are some rules to subnetting:

- ❖ The subnet bits in the IP address cannot be all 1s.
- ❖ The subnet bits in the IP address cannot be all 0s.
- ❖ The host bits in the IP address cannot be all 1s.
- ❖ The host bits in the IP address cannot be all 0s.

When all the host bits are set to 1, the IP address becomes a **broadcast** address. This means that every host on that network will accept the packet for further processing. No host can have a broadcast IP address because it is like a community mailbox address.

When all the host bits are set to 0, the IP address refers to the network and not to any of the hosts. An address with all 0s in the host portion of the address is invalid, and no host can use it.

These rules are easy to follow when using the subnet goggles. Always check out binary IP addresses with the subnet goggles and confirm that neither the **S**s nor the Hs are all 1s or all 0s.

NOTE

RFC 1878 describes a means of subnet addressing that allows for all 1s and all 0s in the subnet bits. Most hardware and software does not support RFC1878 addressing; check the documentation of the hardware or software that you are using.

How to Create a Custom Subnet Mask

The easiest way to create valid subnet masks is to use a **subnet calculator**, (like the one mentioned earlier). Several subnet calculators are available for free on the Internet. To be able to create subnet masks without a subnet calculator is a skill. This skill is useful for certification tests that don't allow calculators. Network administrators also need this skill to set up, troubleshoot, and understand their TCP/IP addressing scheme.

subnet calculator
A software calculator that figures out subnet masks, valid networks, number of hosts, and host ranges. Several are available for download on the Internet.

TIP

Appendix D references the companion Web site for this book. At this Web site, you will find links for downloading some free subnet calculators.

In lieu of using a subnet calculator, an administrator can determine the custom subnet mask by using a simple procedure. The procedure presented in this section is relatively popular and easily understandable. I have found that the more examples I do, the closer I get to mastering this procedure. Get out some paper and a pencil; you'll find that what seems at first difficult will be easy after several repetitions.

There are only six steps to follow in creating a custom subnet mask:

1. Determine how many subnets are needed.
2. Determine the maximum number of hosts on each network.
3. Determine the subnet mask.
4. Determine the valid network addresses.
5. Determine the range of valid host IP addresses on each subnet.
6. Confirm that you met the requirements for the number of networks and maximum number of hosts.

Each of the steps is outlined in the following sections.

Determine How Many Subnets Are Needed

The first step is to determine how many unique subnets are going to be required. A unique subnet address is required on each side of a router where there is not another router on that segment. For example, look at these networks:

WAN connection
A connection between two LANs (local area networks) is a WAN (wide area network) connection.

In the figure above, five unique subnet addresses are required—each on its own side of a router. Notice that although Network B connects to three routers, only one network address is required. Also notice that a unique subnet address is needed for a wide area network (WAN) connection. A **WAN connection** consists of two routers that connect two segments of a WAN.

Determine the Maximum Number of Hosts on Each Network

The second step in figuring out the subnet mask is to find the maximum number of hosts on any of the subnets. For example, if your network has 10 workstations and a router, you'll need 11 host addresses. If your network has 1,000 workstations, 150 TCP/IP printers, and 8 routers, you'll need to plan for 1,158 host addresses on that network. Remember to count the interface to the router as a host.

For the networks illustrated on the previous page, the following number of host IP addresses are required on each network:

Network	Number of Hosts
A	5
B	8
C	2
D	5
E	3

This table shows that the most host addresses needed on any network is eight on Network B.

Determine the Subnet Mask

In this step, you first determine the number of bits you need to take from the host portion of the address to use in the subnet portion, and you then determine the correct subnet mask. You can use either of two methods to figure out how many bits are needed:

Method 1   Calculate

Method 2   Memorize/use a chart

Both are explained in the following sections.

Subnet Masks

Method 1: Calculate

To calculate the number of bits needed to create the proper subnet mask:

1. Add 1 to the number of subnets you need. If you need 8, figure that you need 9. If you need 30, figure 31. If you need 900, figure 901.

2. Convert this decimal number to binary.

Decimal	Binary
9	1001
31	11111
901	11 1000 0101

3. Determine the number of subnet bits that you need: This number is the same as the number of bits that it takes to form the binary number.

Binary	# of Bits
1001	4
11111	5
11 1000 0101	10

4. Add this number to the network portion of the standard subnet mask.

# of Bits	Class A Binary Subnet Mask and Subnet Goggles
4	1111 1111.*1111* 0000.0000 0000.0000 0000
	NNNN NNNN.*SSSS* HHHH.HHHH HHHH.HHHH HHHH
5	1111 1111.*1111* *1*000.0000 0000.0000 0000
	NNNN NNNN.*SSSS* *S*HHH.HHHH HHHH.HHHH HHHH
11	1111 1111.*1111* *1111*.*111*0 0000.0000 0000
	NNNN NNNN.*SSSS* *SSSS*.*SSS*H HHHH.HHHH HHHH

Converted into decimal, these subnet masks are:

# of Bits	Decimal Subnet Mask
4	255.240.0.0
5	255.248.0.0
11	255.255.224.0

Method 2: Memorize/Use Chart

You can use the following table to determine the correct subnet mask:

Max # of Networks Needed	Mask for Subnetted Octet
2	192
3–6	224
7–14	240
15–30	248
31–62	252
63–126	254
127–254	255

Knowing that you will always use **contiguous bits** in the subnet mask, there are only eight possible subnet masks:

# of Bits	Subnetted Octet in Binary	Subnet Mask
1	1000 0000	128
2	1100 0000	192
3	1110 0000	224
4	1111 0000	240
5	1111 1000	248
6	1111 1100	252
7	1111 1110	254
8	1111 1111	255

If you are subnetting more than eight bits, the first eight bits will be set to all 1s, or decimal 255, and the subnetted octet will use this same chart with the remainder of the subnet bits.

Consider this subnet mask:

255.192.0.0 = in binary, 1111 1111.*11*00 0000.0000 0000.0000 0000

There are two subnet bits. This means that IP will look at 10 bits (eight network and two subnet) to determine whether another host is local or remote. The number of networks that can be created with this subnet mask is determined by the number of unique combinations that these two bits can form in the IP address. All possible combinations of these two bits are:

00

01

10

11

However, according to the subnetting rules that you looked at earlier, the subnet bits cannot be all 1s or all 0s. Therefore, only two networks can be created with a subnet mask of 255.192.0.0.

Now consider this subnet mask:

255.128.0.0 = in binary, 1111 1111.*1*000 0000.0000 0000.0000 0000

This subnet mask isn't going to work out because there is only one subnet bit. The possible combinations of the one bit to create unique subnets are:

0

1

Both of these are invalid, because the first is all 0s and the second is all 1s.

Finally, consider the next possible subnet mask:

255.224.0.0 = in binary, 1111 1111.*111*0 0000.0000 0000.0000 0000

Now you have three subnet bits to work with. The possible combinations of these three bits to create unique subnets are:

000

001

010

011

100

101

110

111

This list shows eight unique combinations; however, you have to discard the first and last because of the subnetting rules. This leaves you with six unique subnet addresses.

Determine the Valid Network Addresses

All hosts on each network have to use the same network address, and each network must use a unique network address. The next step in determining an IP addressing scheme is to determine the valid network addresses based on the subnet mask that you decided to use. For every subnet mask, only certain network addresses are valid.

In this step, you determine the first valid network address, and then from that you determine the next valid network addresses.

There is a simple way to determine the valid network addresses for a given subnet mask:

TIP

The decimal value of the subnet mask's rightmost bit that is a 1 is the first network address and the incremental value.

For example, 192 in binary is 1100 0000. The decimal value of the rightmost bit that is a 1 is 64. Therefore, the first network address is 64 and the next network address is 128.

The following chart illustrates this point:

	128	64	32	16	8	4	2	1
SNM = 192	1	1	0	0	0	0	0	0

The next chart continues this illustration. Note the rightmost bit in each subnet mask that is set to 1 (this bit is bold). The rightmost bit in each number corresponds to a decimal value at the top of the chart; this decimal value is the first network number and the incremental value. In this chart's first example, 224 in binary is 1110 0000. The decimal value of the rightmost bit that is a 1 is 32. Therefore, the first network address is 32.

	128	64	32	16	8	4	2	1
SNM = 224	1	1	1	0	0	0	0	0
SNM = 240	1	1	1	1	0	0	0	0
SNM = 248	1	1	1	1	1	0	0	0
SNM = 252	1	1	1	1	1	1	0	0
SNM = 254	1	1	1	1	1	1	1	0
SNM = 255	1	1	1	1	1	1	1	1

For example, say that with the address 131.107.0.0, you would like to create four networks. Following the steps you learned earlier:

1. Add 1 to the number of subnets you need: $4 + 1 = 5$
2. Convert 5 to binary: 101.
3. Because 101 has three bits, you need three bits for the subnet mask. The subnet mask is 255.255.224.0.
4. The rightmost bit set to 1 in 224 has a decimal value of 32. This is the first network number.

Therefore, to create four subnets from 131.107.0.0, you use a subnet mask of 255.255.224.0, and the four networks will be:

131.107.32.0

131.107.64.0

131.107.96.0

131.107.128.0

Why are some network addresses invalid? What about the 131.107.31.0 network? Let's look at the math:

The subnet mask 255.2555.224.0 in binary is the following:

```
1111 1111.1111 1111.1110 0000.0000 0000
```

Using subnet goggles, you have this:

```
            NNNN NNNN.NNNN NNNN.SSSH HHHH.HHHH HHHH
131.107.31.0 = 1000 0011.0110 1011.0001 1111.0000 0000
```

Notice that the subnet bits in the IP address are set to all 0s. This goes against the subnetting rules; therefore, 131.107.31.0 with a subnet mask of 255.255.224.0 is invalid. In this example, this rule applies to all numbers less than 32 in the third octet.

Determine the Range of Valid Host IP Addresses

Only certain addresses will be valid on each of the networks that are created. Therefore, you have to determine the valid IP addresses for each network. In the IP addressing scheme, you must also list the range of valid IP addresses. Finding the range of IP addresses is simple when using the subnet goggles. Simply apply the subnet mask and identify the valid addresses that can be created with the remaining bits. For example, the subnet mask 255.255.224.0 in binary:

> 1111 1111.1111 1111.1110 0000.0000 0000

Using subnet goggles:

> NNNN NNNN. NNNN NNNN.*SSS*H HHHH.HHHH HHHH
> 131.107.32.0 = 1000 0011. 0110 1011.*001*0 0000.0000 0000

The valid, unique host IP addresses on this network are going to be formed from every combination of the last 13 bits. Remember that IP uses the subnet goggles and does not look at the periods. You start with the first address:

> 131.107.32.0 = 1000 0011. 0110 1011. *001*0 0000.0000 0000

This is invalid because it has all 0s in the host.

And then you increase the value of the hosts:

> 131.107.32.1 = 1000 0011. 0110 1011. *001*0 0000.0000 0001
> 131.107.32.2 = 1000 0011. 0110 1011. *001*0 0000.0000 0010
> 131.107.32.3 = 1000 0011. 0110 1011. *001*0 0000.0000 0011

Continue increasing the value of the hosts, and jump ahead to consider:

> 131.107.32.255 = 1000 0011. 0110 1011. *001*0 0000.1111 1111

Is this a valid host IP address? Yes, IP looks at all 13 host bits to see if the host bits are all 1s or all 0s (0000011111111). It can be tricky, but just use the goggles and ignore the periods.

The next IP address in the network can be figured out by again incrementing the 13 host bits by 1, which gives you:

> 131.107.33.0 = 1000 0011. 0110 1011. *001*0 0001.0000 0000

Is this a valid host IP address? Yes, don't forget that IP looks at all 13 host bits (0000100000000), and this address does not have all 1s nor all 0s. So, 131.107.33.0 is a valid host IP address on the 131.107.32.0 network!

Let's continue incrementing the 13 host bits by 1:

> 131.107.33.1 = 1000 0011. 0110 1011. *001*0 0001.0000 0001

131.107.33.2 = **1000 0011**. **0110 1011**. *001*0 0001.0000 0010

131.107.33.3 = **1000 0011**. **0110 1011**. *001*0 0001.0000 0011

Continue to increment the 13 host bits and soon you'll run up to:

131.107.33.255 = **1000 0011**. **0110 1011**. *001*0 0001.1111 1111

Is this a valid host IP address? Absolutely. Look at all 13 host bits (0000111111111). Are they all 1s or all 0s? No, so this is a valid host IP address on the 131.107.32.0 network. Notice that the three subnet bits have not changed.

Continue incrementing the 13 host bits by 1 until you get to:

131.107.63.254 = **1000 0011**. **0110 1011**. *001*1 1111.1111 1110

This is still a valid host IP address on the 131.107.32.0 network. Look at all 13 host bits (1111111111110). Then increment by 1 and get:

131.107.63.255 = **1000 0011**. **0110 1011**. *001*1 1111.1111 1111

Is this a valid host IP address? No, it's not. Look at the 13 host bits (1111111111111). Having all 1s is invalid.

From this exercise, you can conclude that the range of valid host IP addresses on the 131.107.32.0 network with a subnet mask of 255.255.224.0 is:

131.107.32.1–131.107.63.254

The next network starts when you increment the three subnet bits. The next network is going to be:

131.107.64.0 = **1000 0011**. **0110 1011**. *010*0 0000.0000 0000

Now you go through the whole range of unique combinations of the 13 host bits. The range of valid host IP addresses for the 131.107.64.0 network with a subnet mask of 255.255.224.0 is:

131.107.64.1–131.107.95.254

To summarize the example of creating four networks from 131.107.0.0: The subnet mask is 255.255.224.0. The valid networks and host IP address ranges are:

Network	Range of IP Addresses
131.107.32.0	131.107.32.1–131.107.63.254
131.107.64.0	131.107.64.1–131.107.95.254
131.107.96.0	131.107.96.1–131.107.127.254
131.107.128.0	131.107.128.1–131.107.159.254

TEST IT OUT: PUTTING IT ALL TOGETHER, CLASS A

In the following exercise, you will be guided through the process of solving a subnetting problem for a Class A address.

Problem:

Create 1,101 subnets with the Class A address of 10.0.0.0 and find:

1. The subnet mask
2. The first three valid network numbers
3. The range of host IP addresses on those three networks
4. The last valid network and range of IP addresses

Solution:

1. Determine the subnet mask:

   Add 1 to the number of subnets needed: 1,101 + 1 = 1,102

   Determine how many bits are needed for the binary equivalent of the decimal 1,102.

   10001001101 is the binary representation of 1,102 =

   11 bits are needed in the subnet mask

   Standard Class A uses 8 bits + 11 bits = 19 bits needed in subnet mask

   NNNN NNNN.*SSSS SSSS*.*SSS*H HHHH.HHHH HHHH

   Subnet mask = 255.255.224.0

2. Determine the first three valid networks:

   The rightmost subnet bit that equals 1 has a decimal value of 32; therefore, 32 is the first network address and the incremental value.

   First network = 10.0.32.0

   0000 1010.**0000 0000.001**0 0000.0000 0000

   Second network = 10.0.64.0

   0000 1010.**0000 0000.010**0 0000.0000 0000

   Third network = 10.0.96.0

   0000 1010.**0000 0000.011**0 0000.0000 0000

TEST IT OUT: PUTTING IT ALL TOGETHER, CLASS A (cont.)

3. Determine the range of hosts on those three networks:

   For 10.0.32.0 = 10.0.32.1–10.0.63.254

   0000 1010.0000 0000.0010 0000.0000 0001

   0000 1010.0000 0000.0011 1111.1111 1110

   For 10.0.64.0 = 10.0.64.1–10.0.95.254

   0000 1010.0000 0000.0100 0000.0000 0001

   0000 1010.0000 0000.0101 1111.1111 1110

   For 10.0.96.0 = 10.0.96.1–10.0.127.254

   0000 1010.0000 0000.0110 0000.0000 0001

   0000 1010.0000 0000.0111 1111.1111 1110

4. Determine the last valid network and range of addresses:

   NNNN NNNN.*SSSS SSSS*.*SSS*H HHHH.HHHH HHHH

   0000 1010.**1111 1111.110**H HHHH.HHHH HHHH

   The last network = 10.255.192.0

   Range of hosts are:

   0000 1010.1111 1111.1100 0000.0000 0001 = 10.255.192.1

   0000 1010.1111 1111.1101 1111.1111 1110 = 10.255.223.254

In summary:

1. Subnet mask: 255.255.224.0

2. First three valid networks:

   10.0.32.0

   10.0.64.0

   10.0.96.0

3. Range of host IP addresses:

   For 10.0.32.0, 10.0.32.1–10.0.63.254

   For 10.0.64.0, 10.0.64.1–10.0.95.254

   For 10.0.96.0, 10.0.96.1–10.0.127.254

4. Last valid network and host IP address range:

   10.255.192.0 and 10.255.192.1–10.255.223.254

TEST IT OUT: PUTTING IT ALL TOGETHER, CLASS B

In the following exercise, you will be guided through the process of solving a subnetting problem for a Class B address.

Problem:

Create 315 subnets with the Class B address of 172.20.0.0 and find:

1. The subnet mask
2. The first three valid network numbers
3. The range of host IP addresses on those three networks
4. The last valid network and range of IP addresses

Solution:

1. Determine the subnet mask:

    Add 1 to the number of subnets needed: $315 + 1 = 316$

    Determine how many bits are needed for the binary equivalent of the decimal 316.

    100111100 is the binary representation of $316 =$

    9 bits are needed in the subnet mask

    Standard Class B uses 16 bits + 9 bits = 25 bits needed in subnet mask

    NNNN NNNN.NNNN NNNN.*SSSS SSSS*.*S*HHH HHHH

    Subnet mask = 255.255.255.128

2. Determine the first three valid networks:

    The rightmost subnet bit that equals 1 has a decimal value of 128; therefore, 128 is the first network address and the incremental value.

    First network = 172.20.0.128

    1010 1100.0001 0100.**0000 0000.1**000 0000

    Second network = 172.20.1.0

    1010 1100.0001 0100.**0000 0001.0**000 0000

    Third network = 172.20.1.128

    1010 1100.0001 0100.**0000 0001.1**000 0000

TEST IT OUT: PUTTING IT ALL TOGETHER, CLASS B (cont.)

3. Determine the range of hosts on those three networks:

    For 172.20.0.128 = 172.20.0.129−172.20.0.254

    1010 1100.0001 0100.0000 0000.**1**000 0001

    1010 1100.0001 0100.0000 0000.**1**111 1110

    For 172.20.1.0 = 172.20.1.1−172.20.1.254

    1010 1100.0001 0100.0000 0001.**0**000 0001

    1010 1100.0001 0100.0000 0001.**0**111 1110

    For 172.20.1.128 = 172.20.1.129−172.20.1.254

    1010 1100.0001 0100.0000 0001.**1**000 0001

    1010 1100.0001 0100.0000 0001.**1**111 1110

4. Determine the last valid network and range of addresses:

    NNNN NNNN.NNNN NNNN.*SSSS SSSS*.*S*HHH HHHH

    1010 1100.0001 0100.**1111 1111.0**HHH HHHH

    The last network = 172.20.255.0

    Range of hosts are:

    1010 1100.0001 0100.1111 1111.**0000 0001** = 172.20.255.1

    1010 1100.0001 0100.1111 1111.**0111 1110** = 172.20.255.254

In summary, the answers are:

1. Subnet mask: 255.255.255.128

2. First three valid networks:

    172.20.0.128

    172.20.1.0

    172.20.1.128

3. Range of host IP addresses:

    For 172.20.0.128, 172.20.0.129−172.20.0.254

    For 172.20.1.0, 172.20.1.1−172.20.1.254

    For 172.20.1.128, 172.20.1.129−172.20.1.254

4. Last valid network and host IP address range:

    172.20.255.0 and 172.20.255.1−172.20.255.254

Valid Hosts for Class C Addresses

Finding the range of valid hosts with a Class C address is the same process, except that there are so few host bits available that some of the addresses may seem strange. The network portions look like real IP addresses, and the range of valid addresses is as obvious as in the previous examples.

Let's consider the address 192.168.2.0. Say you need 11 networks from this address. You'd take the following steps to find the range of valid hosts:

1. Add 1 to the number of subnets you need: 11 + 1 = 12
2. Convert the result to binary: 1100
3. Because 1100 has four bits, you need four bits in the subnet mask.
   1111 0000 = 240

Subnet mask 255.255.255.240

    = 1111 1111.1111 1111.1111 1111.1111 0000

Using subnet goggles:

    NNNN NNNN.NNNN NNNN.NNNN NNNN.*SSSS* HHHH

The first network address is 192.168.2.16

    = 1100 0000. 1010 1000.0000 0010.*0001* 0000

The valid unique host IP addresses on this network are going to be every combination of the last four bits. Remember, IP uses the subnet goggles and does not look at the periods.

The first address is invalid because it has all 0s in the host:

    192.168.2.16 = 1100 0000. 1010 1000.0000 0010.*0001* **0000**

The next addresses are:

    192.168.2.17 = 1100 0000. 1010 1000.0000 0010.*0001* 0001
    192.168.2.18 = 1100 0000. 1010 1000.0000 0010.*0001* 0010
    192.168.2.19 = 1100 0000. 1010 1000.0000 0010.*0001* 0011
    192.168.2.20 = 1100 0000. 1010 1000.0000 0010.*0001* 0100

Continue increasing the value of the hosts, and jump ahead to consider:

    192.168.2.29 = 1100 0000. 1010 1000.0000 0010.*0001* 1101
    192.168.2.30 = 1100 0000. 1010 1000.0000 0010.*0001* 1110
    192.168.2.31 = 1100 0000. 1010 1000.0000 0010.*0001* 1111

This last address is invalid because it has all 1s in the host portion.

So the first network and range of addresses is:

192.168.2.16 with an IP address range of 192.168.2.17–192.168.2.30

Some of the next networks and their address ranges are:

192.168.2.32 with an IP address range of 192.168.2.33–192.168.2.46

192.168.2.48 with an IP address range of 192.168.2.49–192.168.2.62

192.168.2.64 with an IP address range of 192.168.2.65–192.168.2.94

Using this scheme, 14 subnets can be built, of which you needed only 11.

TIP

To find valid hosts for a Class C network: Find the first network address, and the first valid IP address on that network is one more than the network address. The last valid IP address on that network is the *next* network address minus 2.

To determine the last valid network that can be created with the address of 192.168.2.0 and a subnet mask of 255.255.255.240, let's look at the numbers in their binary representations.

192.168.2.224 = 1100 0000.1010 1000.0000 0010.*1110* **0000**

With an IP address range of:

192.168.2.224 = 1100 0000.1010 1000.0000 0010.*1110* **0001**

through

192.168.2.238 = 1100 0000.1010 1000.0000 0010.*1110* **1110**

The IP address 192.168.2.239 would be invalid because it is the broadcast address on the 192.168.2.224 network:

192.168.2.239 = 1100 0000.1010 1000.0000 0010.*1110* **1111**

If you were to try to create one more network by incrementing the subnet bits by one, you would have:

192.168.2.240 = 1100 0000.1010 1000.0000 0010.*1111* **0000**

Notice that the subnet bits are all 1. That makes this an invalid network address. Always consider the binary representation when determining the validity of addresses.

153

TEST IT OUT: PUTTING IT ALL TOGETHER, CLASS C

In the following exercise, you will be guided through the process of solving a subnetting problem for a Class C address.

Problem:

Create 12 subnets with the Class C address of 192.168.2.0 and find:

1. The subnet mask
2. The first three valid network numbers
3. The range of host IP addresses on those three networks
4. The last valid network and range of IP addresses

Solution:

1. Determine the subnet mask:

   Add 1 to the number of subnets needed: $12 + 1 = 13$

   Determine how many bits are needed for the binary equivalent of the decimal 13.

   1101 is the binary representation of $13 =$

   4 bits are needed in the subnet mask

   Standard Class C uses 24 bits + 4 bits = 28 bits needed in subnet mask

   NNNN NNNN.NNNN NNNN.NNNN NNNN.*SSSS* HHHH

   Subnet mask = 255.255.255.240

2. Determine the first three valid networks:

   The rightmost subnet bit that equals 1 has a decimal value of 16; therefore, 16 is the first network address and the incremental value.

   First network = 192.168.2.16

   1100 0000. 1010 1000.0000 0010.**0001** 0000

   Second network = 192.168.2.32

   1100 0000. 1010 1000.0000 0010.**0010** 0000

   Third network = 192.168.2.48

   1100 0000. 1010 1000.0000 0010.**0011** 0000

TEST IT OUT: PUTTING IT ALL TOGETHER, CLASS C

3. Determine the range of hosts on those three networks:

For 192.168.2.16 = 192.168.2.17−192.168.2.30

1100 0000. 1010 1000.0000 0010.0001 **0001**

1100 0000. 1010 1000.0000 0010.0001 **1110**

For 192.168.2.32 = 192.168.2.33−192.168.2.46

1100 0000. 1010 1000.0000 0010.0010 **0001**

1100 0000. 1010 1000.0000 0010.0010 **1110**

For 192.168.2.48 = 192.168.2.49−192.168.2.62

1100 0000. 1010 1000.0000 0010.0011 **0001**

1100 0000. 1010 1000.0000 0010.0011 **1110**

4. Determine the last valid network and range of addresses:

NNNN NNNN.NNNN NNNN.NNNN NNNN.*SSSS* HHHH

1100 0000. 1010 1000.0000 0010.**1110** HHHH

The last network = 192.168.2.224

Range of hosts are:

1100 0000. 1010 1000.0000 0010.1110 **0001** = 192.168.2.225

1100 0000. 1010 1000.0000 0010.1110 **1110** = 192.168.2.238

In summary:

1. Subnet mask: 255.255.255.240

2. First three valid networks:

192.168.2.16

192.168.2.32

192.168.2.48

3. Range of host IP addresses:

For 192.168.2.16, 192.168.2.17−192.168.2.30

For 192.168.2.32, 192.168.2.33−192.168.2.46

For 192.168.2.48, 192.168.2.49−192.168.2.62

4. Last valid network and host IP address range:

192.168.2.224 and 192.168.2.225−192.168.2.238

Calculating the Number of Networks and Hosts

Now let's look at some of the interesting math solutions of subnetting.

$2^N - 2$

Equation used to figure out the number of subnets and hosts per subnet that can be created with a subnet mask. *N* is the number of bits that you are using for the subnet portion or the host portion of the address.

1. To solve for how many networks you can create, use the equation:

    $(2^N) - 2$ where *N* is the number of subnet bits

    For example:

    A Class B address with a subnet mask of 255.255.240.0 will create $(2^4) - 2 = 14$ networks.

> **TIP**
>
> When using the calculator program that is installed with Windows to solve an exponential equation, click the View option and choose Scientific. Type **2**, click the x^y button, type **4** (or however many subnet bits), type **-**, type **2**.

2. To solve for how many host IP addresses are on each network, use the same equation:

    $(2^N) - 2$ where *N* is the number of host bits

    For example:

    A Class B address with a subnet mask of 255.255.252.0 will allow $(2^{10}) - 2 = 1022$ hosts on each network.

3. To figure out the range of IP addresses on each network, use this two-part equation:

    The first part, or start of the range = (the network address + 1)

    The second part, or end of the range =

    > For Class A, B: (the next network address − 1)

    > For Class C: (the next network address − 2)

    For example, for the network 131.107.2.0 with a subnet mask of 255.255.255.0, the range of IP addresses is 131.107.2.1−131.107.2.254 because:

    > (the network address + 1) = 131.107.2.1

    > through

    > (the next network address, which is 131.107.3.0 − 1) = 131.107.2.254

TEST IT OUT: NUMBER OF NETWORKS AND HOSTS

In the following exercise, you will be shown how to determine the number of networks and hosts given a Class A address and a subnet mask.

Problem

With the Class A address of 10.0.0.0 and a subnet mask of 255.255.224.0, find:

1. How many subnets can be created?

2. How many hosts on each subnet?

Solution:

1. To determine how many subnets can be created:

   Determine how many bits are set to 1 in the custom subnet mask:

   255.255.224.0 has 11 bits set to 1 in the custom portion

   (Standard Class A has 8 bits set to 1)

   Use the $2^N - 2$ equation where $N = 11$

   $2^{11} - 2 = 2,046$

   2,046 unique subnets can be created

2. To determine how many hosts can be on each of those 2,046 subnets:

   Determine how many bits are set to 0 in the subnet mask:

   255.255.224.0 has 13 bits set to 0

   Use the $2^N - 2$ equation where $N = 13$

   $2^{13} - 2 = 8,190$

   8,190 unique hosts can be addressed on each of the 2,046 subnets

Class A Subnet Masks

The table below summarizes all the Class A subnet masks, the number of valid networks, and the number of hosts on each network.

Subnet Mask	# of Unique Valid Networks	# of Hosts On Each Network
255.0.0.0	1—standard subnet mask	16,777,214
255.128.0.0	Invalid—only one bit for subnet portion	—
255.192.0.0	2	4,194,302
255.224.0.0	6	2,097,150
255.240.0.0	14	1,048,574
255.248.0.0	30	524,286
255.252.0.0	62	262,142
255.254.0.0	126	131,070
255.255.0.0	254	65,534
255.255.128.0	510	32,766
255.255.192.0	1,022	16,382
255.255.224.0	2,046	8,190
255.255.240.0	4,094	4,094
255.255.248.0	8,190	2,046
255.255.252.0	16,382	1,022
255.255.254.0	32,766	510
255.255.255.0	65,534	254
255.255.255.128	131,070	126
255.255.255.192	262,142	62
255.255.255.224	524,286	30
255.255.255.240	1,048,574	14
255.255.255.248	2,097,150	6
255.255.255.252	4,194,302	2
255.255.255.254	Invalid—only one bit left for host portion	—
255.255.255.255	Invalid—no bits left for host portion	—

You can memorize this table, or just use the equation $(2^N) - 2$ to figure out any of the entries. The variable N in the equation is the number of subnet bits or the number of host bits.

Class B Subnet Masks

The table below summarizes all the Class B subnet masks and the number of networks and hosts.

Subnet Mask	# of Unique Valid Networks	# of Hosts on Each Network
255.255.0.0	1—standard subnet mask	65,534
255.255.128.0	Invalid—only one bit for subnet portion	—
255.255.192.0	2	16,382
255.255.224.0	6	8,190
255.255.240.0	14	4,094
255.255.248.0	30	2,046
255.255.252.0	62	1,022
255.255.254.0	126	510
255.255.255.0	254	254
255.255.255.128	510	126
255.255.255.192	1,022	62
255.255.255.224	2,046	30
255.255.255.240	4,094	14
255.255.255.248	8,190	6
255.255.255.252	16,382	2
255.255.255.254	Invalid—only one bit left for host portion	—
255.255.255.255	Invalid—no bits left for host portion	—

Class C Subnet Masks

This table summarizes the Class C subnet masks and the number of networks and hosts.

Subnet Mask	# of Unique Valid Networks	# of Hosts on Each Network
255.255.255.0	1—standard subnet mask	254
255.255.255.128	Invalid—only one bit for subnet portion	—
255.255.255.192	2	62
255.255.255.224	6	30
255.255.255.240	14	14
255.255.255.248	30	6
255.255.255.252	62	2
255.255.255.254	Invalid—only one bit left for host portion	—
255.255.255.255	Invalid—no bits left for host portion	—

Review Questions

1. You need to create 652 networks with the Class B address 150.150.0.0.
   a. What is the subnet mask?
   b. List the first three valid network numbers.
   c. List the range of host IP addresses on those three networks.
   d. List the last valid network and range of IP addresses.
   e. How many subnets does this solution allow?
   f. How many host addresses can be on each subnet?

   _____

   _____

   _____

2. You need to create 506 networks with the Class B address 151.151.0.0.
   a. What is the subnet mask?
   b. List the first three valid network numbers.
   c. List the range of host IP addresses on those three networks.
   d. List the last valid network and range of IP addresses.
   e. How many subnets does this solution allow?
   f. How many host addresses can be on each subnet?

   _____

   _____

   _____

3. You need to create 223 networks with the Class B address 152.152.0.0.
   a. What is the subnet mask?
   b. List the first three valid network numbers.
   c. List the range of host IP addresses on those three networks.
   d. List the last valid network and range of IP addresses.

Terms to Know
- ❏ subnet mask
- ❏ local network
- ❏ remote network
- ❏ subnet goggles
- ❏ dotted decimal notation
- ❏ standard subnet mask
- ❏ custom subnet mask
- ❏ subnet
- ❏ subnet bits
- ❏ broadcast
- ❏ subnet calculator
- ❏ WAN connection
- ❏ contiguous bits
- ❏ $2^N - 2$

   e. How many subnets does this solution allow?

   f. How many host addresses can be on each subnet?

_____

_____

_____

4. You need to create 12 networks with the Class C address 200.200.200.0.

   a. What is the subnet mask?

   b. List the first three valid network numbers.

   c. List the range of host IP addresses on those three networks.

   d. List the last valid network and range of IP addresses.

   e. How many subnets does this solution allow?

   f. How many host addresses can be on each subnet?

_____

_____

_____

5. You need to create five networks with the Class C address 201.201.201.0.

   a. What is the subnet mask?

   b. List the first three valid network numbers.

   c. List the range of host IP addresses on those three networks.

   d. List the last valid network and range of IP addresses.

IP address range: 201.201.201.193–201.201.201.222

   e. How many subnets does this solution allow?

   f. How many host addresses can be on each subnet?

_____

_____

_____

6. You need to create 110 networks with the Class C address 202.202.202.0. What is the subnet mask?

_____

7. You need to create 140,000 networks with the Class A address 10.0.0.0. What is the subnet mask?

_____

8. You need to create 54 networks with the Class B address 155.155.0.0. What is the subnet mask?

_____

9. You need to create 110 networks with the Class B address 131.107.0.0. What is the subnet mask?

_____

10. You need to create 425 networks with the Class A address 15.0.0.0. What is the subnet mask?

_____

11. Using the subnet mask of 255.255.0.0 and the Class A address of 10.0.0.0,
    a. How many unique networks can be created?
    b. How many host IP addresses can be on each network?

_____

_____

Chapter

9

Name Resolution

Rather than remember IP addresses, humans find it easier to remember names. Administrators give meaningful names to computers—for example, APPSRVR, ROUTERC, or HARRY. On the Internet, Web sites are given easy-to-remember names such as www.sybex.com. In this way, we can remember names of hosts on our network and of Web sites that we would like to visit.

But TCP/IP cannot find or connect to another computer with just words; TCP/IP needs an IP address. Therefore, the names that we use must be resolved to an IP address before TCP/IP can do anything with them. Resolving—or translating—the name to an IP address is called name resolution. After a name is resolved to an IP address, the host can then figure out whether the destination is local or remote and can continue with the communication. This is similar to finding a phone number when all you know is a name.

In this chapter, you will explore two methods of name resolution:

 Host name resolution

 NetBIOS name resolution

Understanding Name Resolution

name resolution
The process of finding the IP address for the name of a computer.

Name resolution is the process of figuring out the IP address that corresponds to a given name. Because we like to use words for machines, but TCP/IP needs to use IP addresses, we must have a mechanism or method for making the exchange.

For example, the URL for the Sybex Web site is www.sybex.com. This Web site has an IP address of 206.100.29.83. When using a Web browser, it is easier for me to remember www.sybex.com than it is to remember the IP address 206.100.29.83. If I type 206.100.29.83 in my browser, name resolution will not need to take place. I will have already provided the IP address of the Web server that is hosting the Web site that I am trying to connect to. If I use www.sybex.com instead, TCP/IP will need to translate these meaningful words into the IP address.

As an analogy, consider placing a telephone call to a friend. If you want to call a friend and have only his name, the phone call cannot be placed. You need some mechanism to translate his name to a phone number. When translating a friend's name to a telephone number, you have several methods available. You can call the information operator or look in the phone book. Or maybe you have it written down on a piece of paper somewhere, and you just need to find that piece of paper. Which mechanism are you going to use first? Depending on information that you already have, you will use the method that gives you resolution fastest. How many times have you said, "I'll look in this phone book, and if it's not there, I'll call information"?

Similarly, there are several ways to resolve a name to an IP address. Depending on the application that is asking for resolution, the order of these methods that TCP/IP uses is different.

The applications that are going to be asking TCP/IP for resolution fall into two categories. Based on which type of application is asking for resolution, TCP/IP uses either of these two methods:

◆ Host name resolution
◆ NetBIOS name resolution

Each method has several steps. TCP/IP shuffles the order of the name resolution steps for the same reason that you shuffle the order of resolution steps when trying to translate a friend's name to a phone number: speed and efficiency. TCP/IP uses the steps within each of the two categories of name resolution so that the names are resolved to TCP/IP addresses as quickly as possible.

In the same way, you will try all methods that you can think of to match a friend's phone number before giving up—no matter how ridiculous the methods might be.

If you try to get to the Web site ww.sybex.com (notice the typo), TCP/IP will go through the entire host name resolution process before letting you know that there is an error. Resolving www.sybex.com will usually take a maximum of three steps. Depending on the contents of files, resolution might take fewer steps.

If you were a detective trying to find the phone number of a missing person, you would take steps in a particular order to solve the mystery. The order depends on how you think you would get the best results. Similarly, when resolving a name to an IP address, TCP/IP uses the order of steps that has the best chance of resolving the name quickest.

host name resolution
The process of resolving a host name to an IP address.

What Is Host Name Resolution?

The most common method of resolving common names (such as the host name Harry) to IP addresses is **host name resolution**. Most TCP/IP utilities and programs use this method. Host name resolution has seven steps to resolving an IP address. Before reporting an error, TCP/IP will complete each step.

The steps of host name resolution include:

1. Local host
2. HOSTS file
3. DNS
4. NetBIOS name cache
5. WINS
6. Broadcast
7. LMHOSTS file

NOTE

You will learn about each of these steps later in this chapter.

Some of the common utilities and programs that follow the host name resolution method include Ping, FTP, and Web browsers (HTTP).

What Is NetBIOS Name Resolution?

Some Microsoft network applications are written to an **Application Programming Interface (API)** called **NetBIOS**. This means that the programmers used a common interface to help the applications better communicate with the other computers on the network. These programs are referred to as NetBIOS applications.

NetBIOS applications use NetBIOS names, which are also called computer names. By default, the NetBIOS name and host name are the same. To better understand this, imagine that you have a friend who owns a company and you want to look up her telephone number. You can look up the name of the company or the name of your friend—both would reference the same number. Depending on who (which application) is looking for her phone number, a different name is being resolved. If your friend uses her name as the name of the company, the two names would be the same—just as the NetBIOS name and the host name are the same.

The NetBIOS name of a Microsoft computer can be viewed and configured by clicking Control Panel ➢ Network ➢ Identification. When a NetBIOS application needs resolution from a NetBIOS name to an IP address, TCP/IP uses **NetBIOS name resolution**.

The NetBIOS name resolution method has six steps that TCP/IP follows to resolve a NetBIOS name to a TCP/IP address. If these six steps fail to resolve the NetBIOS name to a TCP/IP address, then an error message is displayed to the user.

The steps of NetBIOS name resolution are:

1. NetBIOS name cache
2. WINS
3. Broadcast
4. LMHOSTS file
5. HOSTS file
6. DNS

NOTE

You will learn about each of these methods in this chapter.

Some applications that use the NetBIOS name resolution method include Windows Explorer, NT Explorer, and Microsoft's Net application (which has the net use and net view commands).

Application Programming Interface (API)
A common interface that enables programmers to write programs to a standard specification.

NetBIOS
Network Basic Input Output System; a program that enables applications on different computers to communicate within a local area network.

NetBIOS name resolution
The process of resolving a NetBIOS name to an IP address.

NetBIOS Name Resolution vs. Host Name Resolution

When troubleshooting TCP/IP configuration issues, it is critical to know which method of resolution the application uses. This helps the administrator figure out where resolution is succeeding and failing.

The NetBIOS name resolution and host name resolution methods are basically the same. They include similar steps—but the order that the steps are applied is different. Each method takes a distinct path to resolve names to IP addresses.

The following table lists the order in which the steps are applied in each method.

HOST NAME RESOLUTION	NetBIOS NAME RESOLUTION
Local host (HOSTNAME)	NetBIOS name cache
HOSTS file	WINS
DNS	Broadcast
NetBIOS name cache	LMHOSTS file
WINS	HOSTS file
Broadcast	DNS
LMHOSTS file	

Some of the steps listed in the table are applied only when the computer that is trying to get resolution is using Microsoft's TCP/IP client. Most workstations today have Microsoft's TCP/IP client software installed. There is also a possibility that a TCP/IP client will not be set up to use some of the resolution steps. For example, a client may not be set up to use WINS as a method of resolution. If the client is not set up to use WINS, this step is bypassed.

The orders of resolution are the maps to solving TCP/IP resolution problems. An administrator must be aware of which cycle of resolution to follow when troubleshooting.

Understanding Host Name Resolution

The first category of name resolution to explore is host name resolution. Host name resolution occurs with most TCP/IP utilities and programs. This is the most common method of resolving names to IP addresses.

All TCP/IP hosts have a host name that is configured in the TCP/IP properties of the host. On a Microsoft TCP/IP client, the host name can be viewed and configured by clicking Control Panel ➢ Network ➢Protocol ➢ TCP/IP ➢ DNS. Only Microsoft clients have a NetBIOS name. Remember, the NetBIOS name and the host name are the same by default.

In this section, you will examine each step in the host name resolution process. Let's use the example of pinging www.sybex.com.

The Ping utility is used to confirm that you can use TCP/IP to communicate with another host. The Ping utility uses TCP/IP to send a Ping packet to another host and request that the other host send a response. Before TCP/IP can send a Ping packet, TCP/IP needs an IP address. The TCP/IP stack needs to figure out the IP address of www.sybex.com.

In the illustration below, Harry the Host is going to ping www.sybex.com. Using the Ping utility and a friendly name instead of an IP address will illustrate the need to use host name resolution.

The TCP/IP stack running on the host must resolve the friendly name (www.sybex.com) to an IP address. There are several steps that Harry the host will use to achieve successful resolution. As soon as resolution is successful, the IP address will be passed to the Internet layer of the TCP/IP stack so that IP can determine whether the destination host is local or remote, and communication can commence.

Because Ping falls into the host name resolution category, the steps that the TCP/IP stack running on Harry will follow are:

1. Local host (HOSTNAME)
2. HOSTS file
3. DNS
4. NetBIOS name cache
5. WINS
6. Broadcast
7. LMHOSTS file

Some of these steps refer to Microsoft-specific implementations. Many hosts that today's administrators work with are Microsoft hosts. Any steps that would be skipped by a non-Microsoft host are mentioned as each step is described in the pages that follow.

As you follow the steps involved in host name resolution, keep in mind that all TCP/IP is doing is trying to find the IP address for www.sybex.com. This is similar to trying to find the phone number for somebody when all you have is a name.

As you are learning about host name resolution, also keep in mind the speed with which resolution takes place. You'll be amazed that resolution takes place as fast as it does.

Local Host (HOSTNAME)

The first step in the host name resolution process is to determine whether the local computer (the one that is being used as the source) is also the one that you are trying to reach. This process is known as local host. **Local host** is a method wherein TCP/IP checks to see whether the name of the host that it is on is the same as the host name that it's resolving. Maybe the host that you are sitting at is the host that you are trying to get resolution to. Never overlook the obvious or easiest answer; first check to see whether you are the answer.

In our example, TCP/IP wants to find out whether Harry's name is really www .sybex.com. Harry looks in a mirror to see whether his name is www.sybex.com.

local host
A step in name resolution wherein a host examines its TCP/IP configuration to see whether the name being resolved is its own.

HOSTNAME utility
A simple utility that determines the host name of the computer you are at.

The **HOSTNAME utility** can help answer this question. HOSTNAME is used to discover your host's host name. From a command prompt, type **HOSTNAME** and press Enter. The next line will show you what your host thinks its host name is.

NetBIOS Name Cache

The next step in host name resolution is called NetBIOS name cache, which is used by Microsoft's version of TCP/IP. When using a **Microsoft TCP/IP client**, TCP/IP looks in **NetBIOS name cache**. This is a list in the local host's RAM of the recently resolved NetBIOS names to IP addresses. It's possible that the host name that TCP/IP is trying to get resolution for is also the NetBIOS name of a machine that has recently been resolved.

NetBIOS names that are in cache are like phone numbers that are listed on a scratch piece of paper around the telephone. These pieces of scratch paper have names and numbers that you have recently resolved. They are only temporary and may get thrown away soon.

The following illustration shows Harry checking for the www.sybex.com address on scratch pieces of paper, just like TCP/IP will look in the NetBIOS name cache.

NetBIOS names that have been resolved are placed into NetBIOS name cache for a short amount of time. Before TCP/IP continues with other steps toward resolution, Microsoft's TCP/IP client will stop to see whether this host name is also a NetBIOS name that has already been resolved.

If TCP/IP does not get resolution from NetBIOS name cache, the search continues by using WINS.

Microsoft TCP/IP client

Any TCP/IP host that has installed and configured Microsoft's TCP/IP client software. This accounts for most TCP/IP hosts.

NetBIOS name cache

Temporary cache storage for NetBIOS names and IP addresses that have been resolved.

Scope ID

A NetBIOS scope ID can be configured as a parameter of a Microsoft TCP/IP host. The scope ID segments a physical network into logical networks. If it is important for two hosts on the same network to use the same NetBIOS name, or for two hosts on the same network to be isolated from each other, the scope ID can be used. It is an optional parameter of a NetBIOS and TCP/IP configuration.

When configuring TCP/IP on a Microsoft host, the scope ID field is seldom used. However, in troubleshooting any TCP/IP issues, the scope ID may become an issue if it is in use. When two hosts have different scope IDs, they cannot use NetBIOS to communicate.

On a TCP/IP network, the NetBIOS names are the unique identifiers used by NetBIOS for name resolution. Therefore, no two hosts can have the same NetBIOS name. The scope ID segments the NetBIOS network into different logical networks. For example, in the scope ID field for the host computers in the accounting department, an administrator might type ACCT. These hosts can be identified as HOST1.ACCT or HOST2.ACCT. In another department, the NetBIOS hosts might have a scope ID of SALES. These hosts can be identified as HOST1.SALES or HOST2.SALES.

In these examples, an administrator has created two logical NetBIOS networks, although they are physically on the same network.

However, hosts with a scope ID of SALES cannot access a host with a scope ID of ACCT. Scope IDs must be the same for NetBIOS communication to occur on the same network. Most administrators leave this field blank.

The following screen capture shows the TCP/IP Properties dialog box where the scope ID is set. You set the scope ID in the Network applet of the Control Panel. You access the scope ID from the Control Panel by clicking Network ➢ TCP/IP Properties ➢ WINS Address.

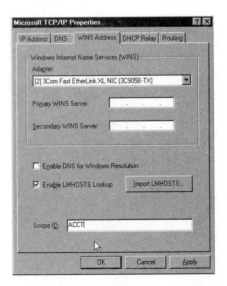

Windows Internet Naming Service (WINS)

The next step in host name resolution is performed only if the host that needs resolution is configured to use **Windows Internet Naming Service** (WINS). A host that is not configured to use WINS will skip this step. WINS is the implementation of a Microsoft NetBIOS name server.

The WINS server keeps a database of all the NetBIOS names and IP addresses of hosts that either register with this WINS server or have been entered into the database manually by an administrator. The administrator configures Microsoft computers on an internetwork to dynamically register their NetBIOS names with the same WINS server. As machines come online, they register with the central WINS server. Now any time another client needs resolution to that NetBIOS name, they ask the special-purpose information operator—WINS—and the operator either returns a positive response with the IP address or a negative response that that name can't be found.

To continue with the analogy, the WINS server acts as a special-purpose telephone information operator. In the illustration below, Harry is asking the local telephone operator for assistance, just like TCP/IP uses WINS.

WINS

Harry

NOTE

For more information on setting up and using WINS, see Chapter 11.

If TCP/IP still has not resolved the name to an IP address, TCP/IP starts getting anxious and tries an almost last-ditch effort.

Windows Internet Naming Service (WINS)
Microsoft's NetBIOS name server that keeps NetBIOS names and IP addresses in a database and later gives name resolution.

Broadcast

Broadcast is another method of name resolution that a TCP/IP client uses. Sometimes the computer name that you are trying to get resolution to is on the same network that you are. The TCP/IP stack will send out a packet that is addressed to all hosts, requesting a response from the host that it is trying to find. The broadcast will go only as far as the router and will not continue to other networks. Therefore, this is a way for TCP/IP to check the local network for resolution. Any response will include the requested host's IP address.

Consider another analogy: If I want to know the phone number of a restaurant, I could open the front door and yell "Hey Denny's, if you can hear me, what is your phone number?" It's possible that Denny's will respond, but chances are I just wasted my time. Denny's is probably not on a residential street; Denny's is on a different street and people there probably can't hear me. By broadcasting, I also wasted bandwidth. Everyone in the neighborhood had to hear me yelling. The broadcast disturbs them momentarily until they realize that the broadcast was not for them. Chances of the broadcast succeeding are better if I yell out the front door for the phone number of one of my neighbors. They live close enough to hear my broadcast and would respond. (They might also decide to move if I did this too often.)

After checking for remote networks, host name resolution is finally checking the local network for resolution. In the following graphic, Harry is broadcasting out the door to try to get resolution.

broadcast
When broadcasting to get name resolution, the host "hollers" the name to be resolved onto the network.

Name Resolution

Broadcasting is an excellent method of name resolution when the computer that you need resolution to is on your local network. If it is not on your local network, the yelling of the broadcast ties up the whole network. The more broadcasts there are on a network, the less **bandwidth** is available for communication. Imagine everyone in your neighborhood constantly broadcasting out their front door to find phone numbers of people and places that don't exist locally. It would just get out of control.

If even after broadcasting TCP/IP cannot get host name resolution, there is one last place to look.

In the screen capture below, notice that Harry sent several DNS queries to his DNS server, through his default gateway. When Harry did not hear back from his DNS server, Harry broadcast three times onto his own network to see if www.sybex.com was on his network.

bandwidth
The amount of data that can move through the cabling.

The *LMHOSTS* file

The **LMHOSTS file** is much like the HOSTS file. It is an ASCII text file that has IP addresses, but instead of containing a host name, the LMHOSTS file contains **NetBIOS names**. The LMHOSTS file does not contain any aliases; it can include only the real NetBIOS name of the computer that you would like resolution to.

The LMHOSTS file is used only on Microsoft's TCP/IP clients that are configured to check the LMHOSTS file. If the client is not a Microsoft TCP/IP client or if the client is not configured to check the LMHOSTS file, this step is skipped.

The LMHOSTS file is similar to a special-purpose phone book that you have at home. For example, in addition to a personal phone book at home, I also have a phone book of all the kids in my son's Little League Baseball team. When I need a number for one of the kids from Little League, I look in the special Little League phone book.

In the following graphic, Harry is looking in a smaller, more specialized phone book, just like TCP/IP looks in the LMHOSTS file.

The LMHOSTS file is located in the same directory as the HOSTS file. To locate the proper directory, see the table in the previous HOSTS file section.

LMHOSTS file
A file containing NetBIOS names and IP addresses that is used for name resolution.

NetBIOS names
The name given to a computer that is running a Microsoft operating system.

NOTE

The *LM* in LMHOSTS stands for **LAN Manager**. Because Windows NT has its roots in a product called LAN Manager, several of the configuration files from LAN Manager are still in use. This is one of those files.

The LMHOSTS file is built with the IP addresses and NetBIOS names of remote computers. Following is an example of an LMHOSTS file:

```
131.107.2.200      INSTRUCTOR      #PRE
131.107.5.22       ACCT_SRV        #PRE
131.107.3.19       FS1
```

Some entries in the LMHOSTS file have switches on the end to enhance their use. The first and second lines above, for example, have a **switch** of #PRE. As the computer boots up and TCP/IP is initializing, TCP/IP will look in the LMHOSTS file for any entries that have #PRE. When TCP/IP finds an entry with #PRE, that entry is immediately pre-loaded into NetBIOS name cache and will stay there indefinitely.

When this TCP/IP stack is trying to resolve a NetBIOS name to an IP address, a name in NetBIOS name cache will be immediately resolved. Therefore, the quickest resolution will always take place if the NetBIOS name and IP address are already in NetBIOS name cache.

The #PRE switch is analogous to me writing some names and numbers on a piece of paper that permanently stays by the phone so that I won't have to go digging through any books to find the number.

The **nbtstat** command is used to view the contents of NetBIOS name cache. There are a few important switches used with the nbtstat command that you should know about. The following table explains the most important switches and their functions.

Switch	Function
-c	Lists what is currently in cache
-R	Purges all entries from name cache and reloads entries that are in the LMHOSTS file that have a #PRE
-n	Lists the NetBIOS names that this machine is known by

LAN Manager
A networking product that was the predecessor of Microsoft's Windows NT.

switch
A character or set of characters used to further enhance a command.

nbtstat
A utility used to monitor the names that are in NetBIOS name cache.

TEST IT OUT: EXAMINING NETBIOS NAME CACHE

In this exercise, you will use the nbtstat utility to view the NetBIOS name cache. Follow these steps:

1. Go to the command prompt by selecting Start ➢ Run and typing **CMD** (Windows NT) or **COMMAND** (Windows 95/98).
2. At the command prompt, type **nbtstat -c** and then press Enter.
3. The screen displays the contents of NetBIOS names and IP addresses that have already been resolved.

Notice in this example that several NetBIOS names have been resolved and are in NetBIOS name cache. TCP/IP examines these for www.sybex.com and will not find it; therefore, name resolution will not be successful at this step.

The nbtstat command can also be used to display the NetBIOS names that this host is currently using. For example, examine the following screen capture. By using the nbstat command with the -n switch, the local NetBIOS names are displayed.

NetBIOS name cache looks like this:

TEST IT OUT: EXAMINING NETBIOS NAME CACHE (cont.)

Notice in the screen shot above that the life remaining for these entries in cache varies. As soon as a NetBIOS name is resolved to an IP address, that entry and its IP address are placed into NetBIOS name cache temporarily. The default is 660 seconds, or 11 minutes. That way, if that machine is used again in the next 11 minutes, name resolution does not need to begin again; the name is already resolved to an IP address. The entry for the machine with the NetBIOS name of ACCT_SRV is −1. Because the entry for ACCT_SRV in the LMHOSTS file includes the switch #PRE, as the TCP/IP stack was loading, ACCT_SRV was placed into NetBIOS name cache with an infinite life, which is represented by −1.

As an administrator, you may add an entry to the LMHOSTS file with the #PRE switch and want to test that it is getting pre-loaded into name cache. Instead of rebooting to reinitialize the TCP/IP stack, a nice shortcut is to use the nbtstat command with the −R switch. When you enter the command nbtstat −R, name cache is purged and all the #PRE-loads are Reloaded.

If after all these methods, TCP/IP still cannot resolve the host name to an IP address, an error message is displayed:

```
Microsoft(R) Windows NT(TM)
(C) Copyright 1985-1996 Microsoft Corp.

C:\>ping ww.sybex.com
Bad IP address ww.sybex.com.

C:\>
```

The Host Name Resolution Cycle

You have examined the seven steps that TCP/IP uses to resolve a name to an IP address. This cycle occurs every time a user tries to connect to another host by using a name instead of an IP address.

When the user of a TCP/IP client uses the name of another host to try to connect, TCP/IP cannot connect with just these words. TCP/IP must have an IP address. If the application uses the host name resolution cycle, which most of them do, the TCP/IP stack will try to resolve the name to an IP address through the seven steps explained earlier. The following illustration depicts a summary of the host name resolution methods.

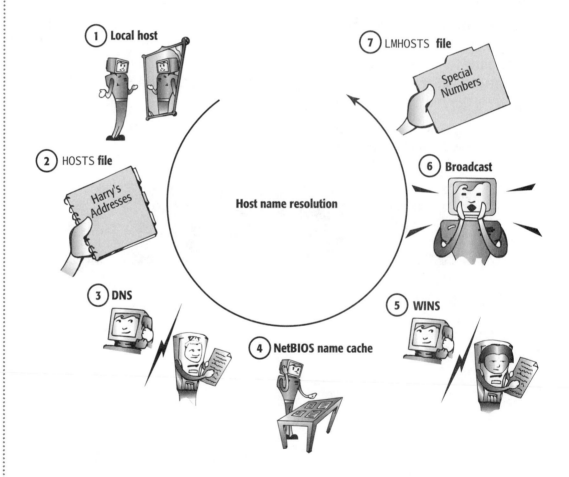

Understanding NetBIOS Name Resolution

Because NetBIOS names are used almost exclusively by a few Microsoft products, the NetBIOS name resolution cycle occurs infrequently. An application that uses NetBIOS names follows essentially the same steps that a TCP/IP application does when using host names to try to get resolution. However, the order in which the steps are tried is different.

The sequence that NetBIOS name resolution uses is as follows:

1. NetBIOS name cache
2. WINS
3. Broadcast
4. LMHOSTS file
5. HOSTS file
6. DNS

As an example, instead of Harry trying to ping `www.sybex.com`, let's have Harry use a Microsoft network application that would cause the NetBIOS name resolution cycle to take place. In this example, the user that is sitting at Harry the Host types in the following command:

```
net view \\instructor
```

This command can be issued when using a Microsoft networked computer, so that the user can view the **shares** that are available on the host with the NetBIOS name `instructor`. The shares are directories on the machine where the contents are shared.

A Microsoft host has a NetBIOS name of 16 bytes, or characters. The first 15 characters are the name of the host. If the computer name is `Harry`, then the first five characters are completed by the name `Harry`. If the computer name is `Instructor`, then the first ten characters are completed by the name `Instructor`. The sixteenth character represents the NetBIOS service that the host is advertising. The characters between the name and the sixteenth character are padded with special characters, usually spaces.

> **shares**
> A feature of several operating systems that is used to designate local resources that will be accessible across the network.

The NetBIOS Name Resolution Cycle

The following illustration shows a summary of the NetBIOS name resolution methods.

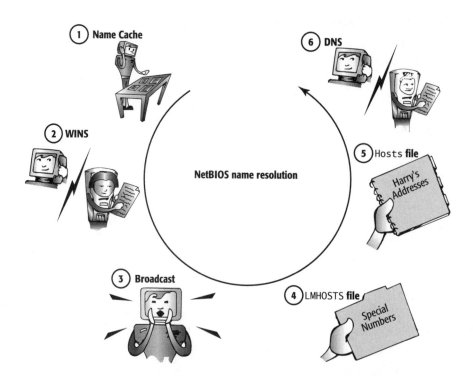

Steps in the cycle occur as follows:

1. Because this application uses NetBIOS names, the first place to look for name resolution is NetBIOS name cache. It's possible that the name has been resolved recently or that it was placed into NetBIOS name cache using the LMHOSTS file.

2. If the NetBIOS name is not in cache, TCP/IP asks the WINS server. If the hosts on this network are set up to use WINS, chances are good that WINS has a listing for the NetBIOS name that this host is trying to get resolution for.

3. If WINS is unsuccessful, or this host is not set up to use a WINS server, TCP/IP broadcasts on the local network to try to get resolution.

4. If the NetBIOS name that is broadcast still does not get resolved, TCP/IP looks in the LMHOSTS file.

5. If the name is not in the LMHOSTS file, maybe it is in the HOSTS file. TCP/IP looks in the HOSTS file next.

6. Finally, if the NetBIOS name is still not resolved, TCP/IP tries DNS.

If any of these methods are successful, the shares on the machine named
`instructor` are displayed. The following screen capture shows the command
and the successful display:

```
Microsoft(R) Windows NT(TM)
(C) Copyright 1985-1996 Microsoft Corp.

C:\>NET VIEW \\INSTRUCTOR
Shared resources at \\INSTRUCTOR


Share name    Type        Used as   Comment
----------------------------------------------------------------
CAP_S00       Disk                  SMS Site S00 CAP 09/28/99
CInfo         Disk
NETLOGON      Disk                  Logon server share
Public        Disk
SMS           Disk
SMS_S00       Disk                  SMS Site S00 09/28/99
SMS_SITE      Disk                  SMS Site S00 09/28/99
SMSLOGON      Disk                  SMS NT logon service
The command completed successfully.

C:\>
```

If none of these methods successfully resolved the NetBIOS name to an IP
address, then an error is displayed for the user. The following screen capture
displays the unsuccessful error message because of the misspelling of *instructor*.

```
Microsoft(R) Windows NT(TM)
(C) Copyright 1985-1996 Microsoft Corp.

C:\>NET VIEW \\INSTRUCTER
System error 53 has occurred.

The network path was not found.

C:\>_
```

Review Questions

Terms to Know
- ❑ name resolution
- ❑ host name resolution
- ❑ API
- ❑ NetBIOS
- ❑ NetBIOS name resolution
- ❑ local host
- ❑ HOSTNAME utility
- ❑ HOSTS file
- ❑ ASCII text file
- ❑ alias
- ❑ parsing

1. What are the two types of name resolution?

2. In the correct order, list the steps of host name resolution.

3. In the correct order, list the methods of NetBIOS name resolution.

4. What is wrong with the following entry in the HOSTS file?

www.sybex.com 206.100.29.83

5. What would be the fastest way to get host name resolution to www.sybex.com?

6. What would be the fastest way to get NetBIOS name resolution to ACCT_SRV?

7. What directory are the LMHOSTS and HOSTS files stored in on a Windows NT workstation?

8. Can you put an alias in the LMHOSTS file?

9. What file and switch are used to place a NetBIOS name into NetBIOS name cache permanently?

_____

10. Write the command you would type to purge NetBIOS name cache and to reload the LMHOSTS file.

_____

11. Which type of name resolution does FTP use?

_____

12. Which type of name resolution does HTTP use?

_____

13. Which type of name resolution will net view use?

_____

14. What is the utility used to check the local host name?

_____

Terms to Know
❏ DNS
❏ Microsoft TCP/IP client
❏ NetBIOS name cache
❏ WINS
❏ broadcast
❏ bandwidth
❏ LMHOSTS file
❏ NetBIOS names
❏ LAN Manager
❏ switch
❏ nbtstat
❏ shares

Chapter

10

Domain Name
System (DNS)

In the preceding chapter, you learned about resolving names to TCP/IP addresses. The top-notch step in resolving host names to TCP/IP addresses is using DNS. The Domain Name System (DNS) is a way to resolve meaningful and easy-to-remember names to IP addresses. Because millions of sites are connected to the Internet, maintaining one central list of the name-to-IP-address relationships across the Internet is unrealistic. The DNS system was designed to coordinate and distribute the resolution load.

The two major tasks that DNS provides are:

◆ IP address resolution to hosts on the Internet, for local hosts

◆ IP address resolution to hosts on the local network, for other hosts on the Internet

In this chapter, you will learn:

 How DNS works

 How a DNS server is set up

 The types of DNS servers

 The types of records in a DNS database

What Is DNS?

As you learned in Chapter 9, **Domain Name System (DNS)** is a distributed database of host names and IP addresses on the Internet. If all the hosts on the Internet were in one big database, that database would be enormous and inefficient. But when the Internet was getting started, the initial idea *was* to keep a file with all host names and their IP addresses in a single file.

In the early days of the Internet, the host names of the sites that were connected to the Internet and their IP addresses were kept in a single file called **HOSTS.TXT**. This file was maintained by the **Stanford Research Institute Network Information Center (SRI-NIC)**. As new hosts were added to the growing network, a simple entry was added to the HOSTS.TXT file with the name and IP address of the new host. If you were one of the hosts on the network, you'd dial into the server at SRI-NIC and download the latest version of the HOSTS.TXT file. When you wanted to connect to another host, you could use the host's name, and TCP/IP would examine the HOSTS.TXT file to translate the name to an IP address.

This is a similar idea to the first phone book that was created. There was only one phone book, and as people hooked up their telephones, their names and numbers were added to the phone book. Everyone who had a phone had to keep getting the updated copy of the phone book. Your phone book was good only if you had a recent copy. Likewise, the HOSTS.TXT file was constantly being updated, and your HOSTS.TXT file was good only if you had a recent copy. An entry was added to or removed from the HOSTS.TXT file only a couple of times a week, so you'd need to download the file only that often to have the latest resolution file.

But as the Internet began to grow, this file became unmanageable. The number of updates to the file and the number of hosts that needed to download the file were growing exponentially. The system was becoming a bottleneck in the name resolution process. Several RFCs were written trying to solve the problem (read RFC 849). In November 1987, the Domain Name System was presented as a solution to the bottleneck; it was outlined in RFCs 1034 and 1035.

DNS on the Internet

Rather than keep all the host names and IP addresses in one unmanageable file, DNS distributes the task across the Internet. All the host names on the Internet are divided into different **domains**, or categories. The top-level domains are categories of host names—for example, commercial organizations are in the .com domain, and educational institutions are in the .edu domain. These top-level domains are further divided into second-level domains, and so on. Examples of second-level domains include sybex.com and microsoft.com.

Each top-level domain maintains a database of the second-level domains. The second-level domains maintain the next layer, and so on. An easy way to get a handle on what the Internet looks like is to view a map of the domain name space. **Domain name space** is the term used to reference how the Internet is subdivided. The top of the domain name space is the root. The root of the domain name space is represented by a period (.).

The illustration below shows a portion of the Internet domain name space. The root is at the top of the domain tree and is represented by a period. The top-level domains contain databases that point to DNS servers for the next layer. For example, the .com DNS server contains entries indicating where to find all the .com DNS servers. The Sybex DNS server contains a database with the host names and IP addresses of hosts and services that the Sybex DNS administrator would like others to get resolution to. For example, it might include entries for www, ftp, and any other names that DNS should provide resolution to.

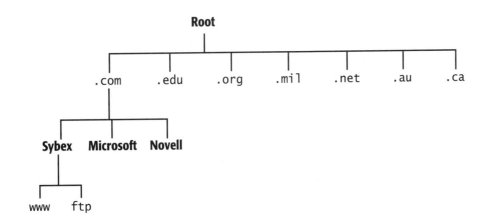

domain
A unique portion of the name space in which an administrator creates an authoritative database of records to give resolution of names within the zone to an IP address.

domain name space
The entire inverted tree of Internet names.

Name Resolution Using DNS

resolver
A client that is trying to resolve a host name to an IP address.

Building a DNS database is similar to building a phone book. When you get a new phone number, you would like people to be able to look up your name in a phone book and get your number. So when you order your phone, you make sure to tell the phone company how you want your name to appear in the phone book. You might also order a second phone line and not want that to be advertised. Your entry appears in a local phone book; putting everyone's name and number in one book would be impossible. Then, if someone wants to resolve your name to a phone number, all they have to do is look in the correct phone book. Because people don't keep a copy of every phone book at home, they don't have access to all phone books, but the information operator does. Information operators can reference all telephone books and resolve names to telephone numbers for a small fee.

DNS provides that special service for its clients on the Internet. When was the last time you saw a commercial advertising the IP address of a Web site? When you sit at a Web browser, rather than type in the IP address of a Web site that you would like to get resolution to, you can type in the name of the Web site and TCP/IP will try to translate that name to an IP address.

When TCP/IP uses DNS as a method of resolution, the host that is trying to get resolution is called a **resolver**. The term *resolver* comes from the Unix world. The resolver sends a message to its DNS server asking for help. The packet says, "Hey, DNS server, can you tell me the IP address for www.sybex.com?"

Imagine, for example, that a user sitting at Harry the Host typed into a Web browser that they'd like to go to www.sybex.com. But with only the words www.sybex.com, Harry cannot get to a Web site. Harry has to have an IP address to send the HTTP request to. He needs to ask Diane, his DNS server, for help.

Querying a DNS Server

Harry knows to ask Diane the DNS Server for resolution help because the administrator who configured Harry's IP address also configured Harry with the IP address of his DNS server. The DNS server can be on the same network or it can be at an ISP. In the illustration below, Harry the Host is the resolver and Diane is the DNS server.

root name servers
Powerful name servers that contain addresses of the top-level name servers.

Harry

Diane

Diane the DNS Server acts as a universal information operator. She receives Harry's request for the IP address of www.sybex.com and first examines what she knows. Diane looks in her database to see whether she can answer Harry's question with no outside assistance. If Diane can answer his question, she'll send the IP address to Harry, and resolution is complete. Harry will then send an HTTP request to the IP address given to him by Diane the DNS Server.

If Diane does not know the answer, she will need to get some outside assistance. She asks a **root name server**. There are 13 root name servers. These are strategically placed name servers that contain the IP addresses of the top-level domain name servers. Every DNS server has the IP addresses of all these root name servers automatically installed to their local database. Therefore, every DNS server can ask any of the 13 root name servers for resolution.

Querying Name Servers

Since Diane the DNS Server has the IP address of the root name servers, she can start the process of name resolution. The first thing that little ol' Diane, a DNS server from some little network that nobody knows about, will do is ask one of these enormous and powerful root name servers if they know the IP address of www.sybex.com. See the illustration below.

The root name servers have IP addresses of the top-level domain name servers. So the root name server responds to Diane and says "No, I don't know www.sybex.com, but I do have the address for .com." The root name server sends back the best information it has.

Now Diane has the address of a .com server. She takes that information and caches it. Diane will keep this information in **cache** as long as was specified by the DNS administrator of the DNS server that provided the information. Diane caches that address of .com because sometime soon she may be asked again for resolution to a URL that is in the .com domain. With the address cached, she won't have to bother the root name server with the same question.

Using the address she obtained, Diane sends a request to the .com name server and asks for resolution to www.sybex.com. The .com name server does not have the IP address of www.sybex.com, but does have the IP address of sybex.com. The .com name server sends a response to Diane that says, "I don't know the IP address of www.sybex.com, but I do know the address of sybex.com."

In the illustration below, Diane the DNS Server sends a request to the .com name server asking for resolution to www.sybex.com. The .com name server responds with the IP address of sybex.com.

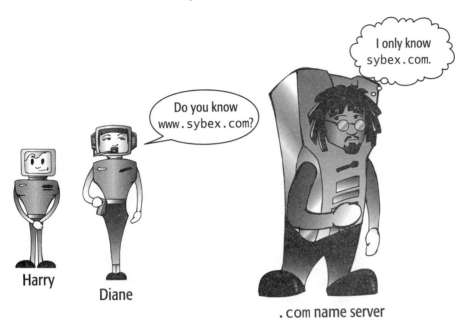

When Diane the DNS Server receives the response from the .com server, she caches the IP address of sybex.com. Diane then sends a request to the IP address of sybex.com asking for resolution to www.sybex.com.

The DNS server at sybex.com has the address of www.sybex.com. The sybex.com name server responds, "Yes, I do have the IP address for www.sybex.com; here it is." See the illustration below.

Completing Resolution

Now that Diane the DNS Server has the IP address for www.sybex.com, she caches the IP address and then sends a packet to Harry. In this response to Harry, Diane sends the IP address of www.sybex.com. Now that Harry has the address, Harry's TCP/IP stack sends an HTTP request to the IP address sent by Diane.

With all these pieces of resolution cached, Diane has part of the work (or possibly all of the work) already completed if another resolver asks her for resolution to anything in .com, or anything at sybex.com, or at www.sybex.com.

The screen capture below shows a packet that is sent from a host named Harry to a DNS server. The packet is a DNS query for www.sybex.com. In the DNS question section of the packet, which is highlighted, you can see the question being asked is "What is the IP address of www.sybex.com?"

Understanding Recursive and Iterative Queries

After a query has been sent from the resolver to the DNS server, the DNS server responds with either the IP address or an error. The DNS server hides the work that has to take place to get name resolution. The query that the resolver sends to the DNS server is called a **recursive query**. A recursive query means: Give me the answer or give me an error, but don't give me anything in between.

The DNS server then asks other name servers to help with resolution. The query that a DNS server sends to another name server is called an **iterative query**. An iterative query asks for the best you've got: If you don't have the answer to the whole question, please give me any resolution that you can help with. The iterative queries may be repeated several times while the DNS server just keeps asking other name servers, "Help me as much as you can." That is why other name

---

recursive query
A question asked with the expectation that the response will be either the complete answer or an error, nothing less.

iterative query
A question asked with the expectation that the best information available will be returned so that more queries can be sent based that information.

servers will respond with the best that they do know. The iterative queries are hidden from the resolver; the resolver wants resolution but does not care how many name servers are helping with resolution.

The screen capture below shows the packet that is returned to Harry with resolution to www.sybex.com accomplished. Based on this response, Harry the resolver does not know how resolution occurred; he just gets the resolution he asked for—the IP address shown at the bottom of the screen capture. The packet shows both the question that was asked and the answer.

The DNS server might not be able to resolve the request. For example, imagine that Harry asks for resolution to fs1.sybex.com. The DNS server can resolve sybex and .com but cannot resolve fs1, so only an error is returned to Harry. The screen capture below shows the error being returned to Harry from the DNS server. The response says that the name fs1.sybex.com does not exist.

Maintaining a Database

One major task of the DNS server is to provide resolution for the resolvers that are configured to use that DNS server. Another major task is to maintain a database of host names and IP addresses. Then, when a query is made of the DNS server, it first looks in its database to see whether it can help with resolution. The administrator of a DNS server has to type in the host names and IP addresses in the database that the DNS server uses in resolving requests.

For example, an administrator for the sybex.com DNS server made an entry into a database at that server that www.sybex.com has the IP address of 206.100.29.83. After my DNS server got resolution to sybex.com, it queried the sybex.com DNS server for the IP address of www.sybex.com. The sybex.com DNS server responded with the correct address.

The .com server has an entry in its database that points any query for *any-thing*.sybex.com to the sybex.com DNS server. The sybex.com DNS server has the information needed to give resolution to *(anything the administrator wanted)*.sybex.com. The DNS administrator at Sybex typed these entries in the sybex.com DNS server's database, which is stored as a zone file. The administrator is in charge of the zone, and more specifically the zone file, for sybex.com. A zone file contains the names and IP addresses for this particular part of the domain name space. The administrator puts the records for sybex.com into a zone file called sybex.com.dns.

DNS is a service that can be run on different platforms and operating systems. The database that each DNS server uses is made of several files. Most DNS versions and implementations follow a standard called the Berkeley Internet Name Domain (BIND) implementation. The BIND implementation describes what files are necessary and what information the records in the DNS database must include.

Every DNS administrator maintains a DNS database. These databases are linked through the Internet to create a network of DNS databases. The DNS servers than work together to provide name-to-IP-address resolution and IP-address-to-name resolution. Because every administrator is maintaining their own database, and all the databases work together, successful DNS resolution is a collaborative effort.

Maintaining a DNS Server

A DNS administrator sets up and maintains the DNS database. DNS server software can be run on several operating systems. Depending on the operating system that is chosen, the administration methods differ slightly, but the basic concepts are the same. A server that the DNS service is run on is called a **name server**. There are three types of name servers, which are described in the following sections.

Primary Name Server

The **primary name server** holds the **master DNS database**. The administrator makes all updates to the master DNS database. The primary name server holds a **read/write** copy of the database. To add, delete, or modify any of the records in the DNS database, the administrator accesses the primary name server and modifies the master DNS database.

A primary name server is like an information operator with the master phone listing for her area. All modifications are made to this master phone listing. With just one copy of the DNS database on the primary name server, name resolution will take place just fine. However, an administrator has the option to assist the primary name server by setting up a **secondary name server**.

Secondary Name Server

A secondary name server holds a copy of the DNS database. This server provides resolution in the same way that the primary name server does.

Secondary name servers assist the primary name servers. Administrators set up secondary name servers for the following reasons:

Fault tolerance If one server goes down or is unavailable, the other name server will be able to handle name resolution queries.

Load balancing If a server becomes overloaded with name resolution requests, another name server will lighten the load.

Remote resolution If you need to resolve an IP address from a remote site, a secondary name server can be placed at the remote location so that resolution can take place at that location without having to continually send traffic across WAN links.

---

name server
A server running the DNS service that can provide name resolution.

primary name server
The name server that holds the master DNS database.

master DNS database
The authoritative DNS database containing DNS records, where the administrator can modify records.

read/write
A file that can be read from and written to.

secondary name server
A name server that has a copy of the master DNS database.

fault tolerance
Taking into account any failures.

load balancing
Spreading the workload across servers.

203

DNS Zone Transfer

The secondary name server receives a copy of the master DNS database from the primary name server. The administrator does not make changes to the database on the secondary server; all updates must be made at the primary name server only. The secondary name servers hold a **read-only** copy of the DNS database. When the primary name server is updated, a copy of that database (zone file) is transferred to the secondary name servers.

Continuing the analogy of the information operator, the secondary name server is like another information operator. The second information operator gets a copy of the master phone list and can use it but can't update it. The second information operator helps with resolution just like the primary operator does.

The transfer of the database is called a **zone transfer**. A zone transfer moves the database from the primary name server to the secondary. Whenever a secondary name server comes online, it automatically initiates a zone transfer. The administrator also can set up a zone transfer to occur from a secondary to another secondary. The first transfer has to be from the primary name server to a secondary; then that secondary may transfer the database to another secondary.

The illustration below is an example of a DNS database being transferred. The primary name server performs a zone transfer to two secondary name servers, and one of the secondary name servers performs a zone transfer to a third secondary.

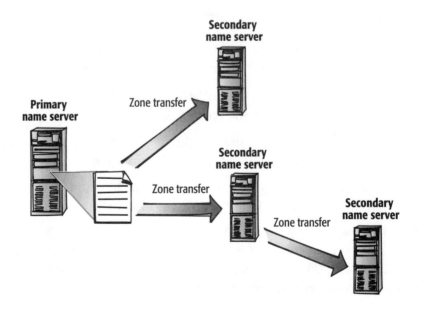

read-only
A file that can be read but cannot be modified.

zone transfer
The sending of a DNS database from one name server to another.

Caching-Only Server

A **caching-only server** contains no database. When the caching-only server comes online, it knows nothing. When the first query comes to it for resolution, the caching-only server must start at the root and work out all the levels of resolution. After it has resolved a URL, it has some information cached for the next query. The caching-only server quickly learns and caches the most commonly resolved queries. The caching-only server requires little setup and virtually no maintenance. When any DNS server is initially installed, it is essentially a caching-only server until you add the zone database.

A caching-only server is like an information operator not having a phone book. When the operator starts working, she must ask other operators for assistance on every query. As she resolves numbers, she jots notes to herself and gradually builds her own Rolodex. Soon she has the most frequently asked for names already resolved and handy.

Caching-only servers are excellent choices for remote offices connected by WAN links. Because there is no zone transfer when the caching-only server comes online, there is no initial bandwidth consumption.

caching-only server
A name server that does not have a copy of a DNS database.

records
The information in the DNS database.

Record Types in DNS

The DNS database is a collection of **records**. Several types of records can be included in the DNS database. The records are like cards in a Rolodex file. The first card describes the data in the Rolodex; it might contain the information about whose Rolodex it is and when it was created. Most cards in the Rolodex have a name, address, and phone number. The Rolodex might also include some other cards with various functions.

Some of the most common record types are:

- ◆ Start Of Authority (SOA) record
- ◆ A record
- ◆ CNAME record
- ◆ NS record
- ◆ PTR record
- ◆ MX record

Each is described in the following sections.

Common Record Types

Start Of Authority (SOA) Record

A DNS database starts with a record called an **SOA record**. SOA stands for Start Of Authority, and there is only one SOA record in each zone database file. This record describes the zone in the domain name space that a particular database is authoritative over. In the Rolodex example, this would be the card that describes the card file, who it belongs to, when was it last updated, and other information about the data. In the Sybex DNS database, the SOA record describes the sybex.com zone, which is the zone that the Sybex database is authoritative over.

A Record

An **A record** is also called a Host record. This is the most common record type in a DNS database. The A record contains host names and IP addresses. This is like the cards in a Rolodex that have the actual names, addresses, and phone numbers.

CNAME Record

The term **CNAME** stands for Canonical name. Even though it has a fancy name, the record is simply a *code* name for an A record. Canonical names are aliases that have been entered into the DNS database. These records provide different ways to reference host records that are already in the database.

For example, say an administrator wants people to be able to get resolution to both fs1.sybex.com and www.sybex.com. Both have the same IP address. The DNS database already has an A record for www.sybex.com. So the administrator simply puts a CNAME record into the database for fs1 that points to the www A record.

In the Rolodex example, a card might be added for someone, and the card simply has a name and a note to go look at another card for the address or phone number. If my friend's nickname is "Pony," I can have a card that says "Pony" that points to the original card with his real name and number.

NS Record

An **NS record** indicates this and other name servers that are being used by this name server. An NS record exists for every name server that services the domain. Using the information operator analogy, an NS record has the phone number of all the operators that are using a copy of a particular phone book. This information will help them to contact each other.

PTR Record

A **PTR record** is used so that a query for the host name, not the IP address, can be resolved. If a query comes to the DNS server that says, "Here is the IP address; what is the host name?" the PTR record provides resolution. Every time an A record is added to the DNS database, a PTR record should also be added.

This would be similar to looking at a phone book and asking, "I have this phone number; whose number is it?" Or a modern example is the caller-ID feature that is available for your telephone. This service displays the name of the person who is calling as well as their phone number. If all it displayed were a telephone number, it would be an almost useless feature. It's when a reverse lookup is done and the name is displayed that the benefits of this call screening feature are realized.

Few applications are written that request a host name (the application knows the IP address, but would like to know the host name). The query that these applications send to the DNS server is called a reverse, or inverse, query. The DNS server examines the PTR records and responds with the host name that corresponds to the IP address. These PTR records are in a special zone called the **IN-ADDR.ARPA** zone. When a query comes to the DNS server requesting an inverse lookup, the DNS server can look in the IN-ADDR.ARPA zone for quick resolution.

MX Record

An **MX record** is a Mail eXchanger record. This record has the IP address of the server where e-mail should be delivered. For example, when e-mail is sent to andy@sybex.com, the DNS server at Sybex is queried for the address of the mail server at sybex.com. The DNS server looks for any MX records for sybex.com and returns the IP address of the mail server to where the mail should be transferred.

Other Record Types

An administrator could use other record types for their DNS database. Examples of such records include a WKS record that points to a Well Known Service or an RP record that indicates the Responsible Person for the database. The most common records, however, have been presented in this chapter.

Pointer (PTR) record
A record that aids with IP address-to-host-name resolution.

IN-ADDR.ARPA
Inverse Address from the ARPAnet; a zone used to keep PTR records.

Mail eXchanger (MX) record
A record that contains the address of the mail server.

Review Questions

Terms to Know
- ❏ DNS
- ❏ HOSTS.TXT
- ❏ SRI-NIC
- ❏ domain
- ❏ domain name space
- ❏ resolver
- ❏ root name servers
- ❏ cache
- ❏ recursive query
- ❏ iterative query
- ❏ name server
- ❏ primary name server
- ❏ master DNS database
- ❏ read/write

1. What is the name of the original file used to store host names and IP addresses?

    _____

2. What RFCs describe DNS?

    _____

3. What character represents the root of the domain name space?

    _____

4. What is the client called when asking for resolution?

    _____

5. How does the client know the IP address of the DNS server?

    _____

6. What type of query does the client send to the DNS server?

    _____

7. What type of query does the DNS server send to other name servers?

    _____

8. List three types of name servers.

    _____

    _____

    _____

9. What is the term used when a DNS database is copied from one name server to another?

_____

10. Can a secondary name server copy the DNS database to another secondary name server?

_____

11. Can a secondary name server copy the DNS database to a caching-only name server?

_____

12. What is the most common record type in a DNS database?

_____

13. What is the process of resolving an IP address to a host name called?

_____

Terms to Know
- ❑ secondary name server
- ❑ fault tolerance
- ❑ load balancing
- ❑ read-only
- ❑ zone transfer
- ❑ caching-only server
- ❑ records
- ❑ SOA record
- ❑ A record
- ❑ CNAME record
- ❑ NS record
- ❑ PTR record
- ❑ IN-ADDR.ARPA
- ❑ MX record

Chapter

11

Windows Internet Naming Service (WINS)

I n the previous chapters, you learned that most applications are written to use host names and host name resolution. You also learned that some applications are written to use NetBIOS names and NetBIOS name resolution. In this chapter, you will learn more about a NetBIOS name resolution service provided by Microsoft called Windows Internet Naming Service.

WINS is a local database of NetBIOS names and IP addresses. The WINS service provides resolution from the WINS database to its clients when a NetBIOS name to IP address resolution is needed.

In this chapter you will learn about:

   NetBIOS applications

   NetBIOS name resolution without WINS

   NetBIOS name resolution with WINS

   WINS Manager

NetBIOS Applications

Many networks today are made up of a combination of workstations that use Windows 95/98, Windows NT, or Windows 2000 as their desktop operating system. A handful of applications have been written that use the NetBIOS names of these hosts instead of their host name. For example, a user on a network can open an application called Network Neighborhood and see the names of other workstations and servers. Network Neighborhood displays the NetBIOS names of other hosts.

workstation service
A NetBIOS service that performs workstation activities such as using the local operating system.

server service
A NetBIOS service that performs server activities such as file sharing.

When a Microsoft host is starting and building its TCP/IP stack, several NetBIOS services begin. These NetBIOS services will provide a service either to the local host or to other hosts in the network. Some of the NetBIOS services that a host may provide include the **workstation service** and the **server service**.

These services are like applications that are running on the host. The host automatically starts these services and offers them to other hosts. For example, the server service enables other hosts to connect to and share files from the host that is offering the service. The NetBIOS name and the service that are being offered must be unique on the network; no other host can be offering the same NetBIOS name and service.

NetBIOS Name Resolution Process without WINS

A computer's NetBIOS name needs to be resolved to an IP address for TCP/IP to communicate with that host. If the host cannot resolve the NetBIOS name to an IP address, communication will not occur. NetBIOS name resolution was developed many years ago for use without WINS. Microsoft TCP/IP clients can still use NetBIOS name resolution without WINS. However, WINS offers several improvements that you will learn about later in this chapter.

Name Registration

Before NetBIOS name resolution can take place, the NetBIOS hosts must go through a process of registering their NetBIOS names. The process of NetBIOS name resolution begins when a TCP/IP host that is running NetBIOS services starts; the host broadcasts a NetBIOS name registration packet that includes its NetBIOS name and the service that it offers. If any other host on the network receives the broadcast and has the same name, it sends back a **negative acknowledgment**. The registering host listens for any negative acknowledgments, and if none are received, the host assumes that it has a unique name. However, if a negative acknowledgment is returned, an error message is displayed telling the user that the NetBIOS name is already in use.

In the following screen capture, a name registration packet is being broadcast onto the network to register the NetBIOS name Harry. Notice that the name registration packet is *broadcast* from Harry.

As all the hosts come online and broadcast their NetBIOS names and services, there will be no duplicates. The host may be offering several NetBIOS services and will broadcast each. On a network, the second host that wants an existing NetBIOS name would not be able to start any NetBIOS services that already existed on the network. When a host powers down, or leaves the network, that NetBIOS name becomes available because another host can then come online and broadcast that name, and the original name holder will not be online to generate a negative acknowledgment.

Suppose there is a conference and a requirement of the conference is that no two people have the same name. As new members walk into the conference room, they broadcast their names. Harry walks in, and in a very loud voice broadcasts, "I am Harry." All the other conference attendees examine their name tags to see whether their name is Harry. If someone else named Harry is already in the room, he'd yell back, "Sorry Harry, I'm already here." Harry the newcomer would not be allowed to participate in the conference. As more people enter the conference room, they continue broadcasting their names, and the other attendees examine their name tags to make sure that there are no conflicts.

negative acknowledgment
An acknowledgment sent from a host or server that says "I received your request and the answer is no."

213

The Conference—Name Registration without WINS

The illustration below shows Harry walking into a conference room and broadcasting that his name is Harry. The others check their name tags for any conflicts. Again, this is analogous to NetBIOS name registration.

NetBIOS name cache

Recently resolved NetBIOS names and IP addresses stored in RAM for rapid resolution.

NetBIOS name query

A packet asking for the IP address of a host with a particular NetBIOS name.

Name Resolution

Now you have learned how NetBIOS name registration takes place, the next issue is name resolution. When a host on a network wants to communicate with another host that is using a NetBIOS application, the initiating host uses the NetBIOS name resolution methods as described in Chapter 9.

The first place to look for NetBIOS resolution is in the **NetBIOS name cache**. Possibly the name was recently resolved or was configured with the LMHOSTS file to be permanently in NetBIOS name cache. If the NetBIOS name is not in NetBIOS name cache, and the host is not configured for WINS, a **NetBIOS name query** is broadcast.

The NetBIOS name query packet contains the NetBIOS name in question and the IP address of the originator. The name query is broadcast to the network asking for the owner of the name to respond with an IP address.

The screen capture below shows a host named Sally broadcasting a name query request (Query Req) for a node named Harry. Notice that the packet source is SALLY and the destination is addressed to BROADCAST.

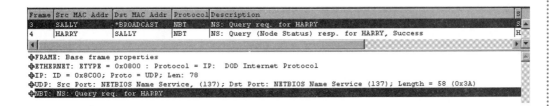

Each host examines itself as the name query broadcast is received. When the owner of the name recognizes itself as a match, a name query response is sent back to the originator of the query. The response includes the NetBIOS name and IP address of the destination. Now that the originator has the IP address of the destination, TCP/IP will begin the communication process with the destination.

The following screen capture shows the positive response that Harry sends back to Sally with his IP address in the last line of the screen capture. The source of the packet is Harry, and the destination is Sally.

To continue with the example of the conference, suppose that everyone in the conference has a separate telephone. When one person wants to talk to another at the conference, the only way to get the other person's number is to broadcast for the person. If Sally wants to have a communication with Harry, she just shouts in the conference room, "Hey Harry, what's your number? My number is x531." As everybody in the room hears that name query broadcast, they examine their name tags. When Harry recognizes that Sally must be talking about him, Harry picks up his phone and calls x531. He says, "This is Harry. I understand that you want to talk with me; my number is x220." Now Sally, the originator of the name query, has Harry's telephone number and is able to begin communicating.

The Conference—Name Registration without WINS

The following illustration shows Sally shouting for Harry in the same way that NetBIOS name queries are broadcast.

network bandwidth
The amount of data that can be put onto a network based on other communication traffic already using the wire.

This process of NetBIOS name resolution is efficient and works fine on a small network. As the network grows, however, this method becomes unacceptable. Imagine the conference in the preceding example with 10 people in the conference room. The number of broadcasts in the room would be acceptable and probably an efficient method of name-to-number resolution. If the coordinators of the conference decided to give free food and suddenly 1,000 people attended, the number of broadcasts would be out of control. Broadcast would then be an unacceptable and inefficient method of name resolution.

As networks got larger and it became obvious that broadcasting for NetBIOS name resolution was inefficient and consuming a great deal of **network bandwidth**, a solution was developed to rectify the problem. Imagine that conference room with 1,000 people and try to think of a more efficient way for people to get name resolution to one another's numbers.

NetBIOS Name Resolution Process with WINS

To decrease the inefficiency of using broadcasts to resolve NetBIOS names, the **NetBIOS name server** was created. A NetBIOS name server contains a dynamic database of NetBIOS names and IP addresses. WINS is a service that acts as a NetBIOS name server. The WINS service can be installed on a Windows NT server.

The IP address of the WINS server must be configured for any hosts that will use that WINS server. Since the administrator might not use a WINS server, the WINS IP address is an optional parameter of the TCP/IP configuration. An administrator can manually enter the IP address of the WINS server for every host, or if the network is set up to use DHCP, the WINS server address can be set up as an optional parameter that is supplied with the automatic IP address.

Name Registration

For a TCP/IP client that is configured to use WINS, the process of name registration changes a bit. Now, as the host is connecting to the network, rather than broadcast a name registration packet, the host sends a name registration packet directly to the WINS server. The name registration packet includes the NetBIOS name, IP address, and the NetBIOS services that the host is registering. The WINS server looks in the database to see whether another host has already registered that NetBIOS name. If there are no other entries with that NetBIOS name, the WINS server sends a positive acknowledgment back to the host.

Using WINS for name-to-IP-address resolution is similar to having a registrar at the conference described earlier in this chapter. The illustration below shows Rita the Registrar at the conference. Rita will handle registrations and resolutions.

NetBIOS name server
A server that registers and resolves NetBIOS names.

If you have any questions, ask Rita.

Rita
Registrar of Conference

Jim

Susan

Martha

Name Registration with WINS

The following screen capture shows a name registration request for the NetBIOS name Harry. The name registration is not broadcast; it is sent directly to the WINS server. The registration packet includes the name to be registered and Harry's IP address. Also in the screen capture, the second captured packet (frame 10) is the WINS server's positive response to Harry.

```
Frame  Src MAC Addr  Dst MAC Addr  Protocol  Description                                                      S
9      HARRY         WINS SERVER   NBT       NS: Registration req. for HARRY           <00>                   H
10     WINS_SERVER   HARRY         NBT       NS: Registration (Node Status) resp. for HARRY      <00>, Success W

 ⊕ FRAME: Base frame properties
 ⊕ ETHERNET: ETYPE = 0x0800 : Protocol = IP:  DOD Internet Protocol
 ⊕ IP: ID = 0x100; Proto = UDP; Len: 96
 ⊕ UDP: Src Port: NETBIOS Name Service, (137); Dst Port: NETBIOS Name Service (137); Length = 76 (0x4C)
 ⊖ NBT: NS: Registration req. for HARRY           <00>
    NBT: Transaction ID = 32768 (0x8000)
 ⊕  NBT: Flags Summary = 0x2900 - Req.; Registration; Success
    NBT: Question Count = 1 (0x1)
    NBT: Answer Count = 0 (0x0)
    NBT: Name Service Count = 0 (0x0)
    NBT: Additional Record Count = 1 (0x1)
    NBT: Question Name = HARRY           <00>
    NBT: Question Type = General Name Service
    NBT: Question Class = Internet Class
    NBT: Resource Record Name = HARRY           <00>
    NBT: Resource Record Type = NetBIOS General Name Service
    NBT: Resource Record Class = Internet Class
    NBT: Time To Live = 300000 (0x493E0)
    NBT: RDATA Length = 6 (0x6)
 ⊕  NBT: Resource Record Flags = 24576 (0x6000)
    NBT: Owner IP Address = 209.132.94.100
```

If the WINS server finds that a host has already registered that NetBIOS name, the WINS server sends a challenge. Three challenge packets are sent to the IP address of the host that registered that name. The challenge packets are simply asking, "Hey, are you still there?" If the host responds that it is still there and online, a negative acknowledgment is sent back to the other host that is requesting the registration. That host will then get an error message that a duplicate NetBIOS name exists. If the challenge goes unanswered, then the WINS server has to assume that the original host is no longer there. The server then updates the WINS database and sends a positive acknowledgment to the host requesting the registration.

If a host sends a name registration request to the WINS server and the WINS server does not respond, the host will resend the request up to three times before giving up. If the host gets no response from the WINS server after three tries, the host broadcasts the name registration request and listens for other hosts to send a negative acknowledgment. Therefore, when the new, better WINS service doesn't seem to be working, the client will go to the name registration method as if WINS didn't exist.

When we apply the WINS server to our conference example, name registration becomes a simple process. As people enter the conference room, they simply tell the registrar their names. As Harry comes into the conference, the registrar looks through the conference registration database and confirms that no one else in the conference is named Harry. If someone already has registered that name, the registrar calls their number and confirms that they are still at the conference. If no one answers at that number, the registrar will try two more times to be absolutely sure that they are no longer at the conference. If after three tries there is still no answer, the registrar updates the registration database with Harry's information and welcomes the new Harry to the conference with a positive name registration acknowledgment.

The illustration below shows Harry registering for the conference and the registrar looking at the database for any conflicts. Again, this is similar to NetBIOS name registration with WINS.

Harry

Rita
Registrar of Conference

Name Resolution

When using WINS, NetBIOS name resolution is a simple process that begins by sending the WINS sever a name query. Instead of broadcasting, a host that is trying to get NetBIOS name resolution simply sends a name query to the WINS server. The WINS server examines the WINS database and sends back either a positive or a negative response.

If the NetBIOS name being requested exists in the WINS database, the NetBIOS name and IP address are returned to the originator of the name query. This is a positive name query response. The host now has the IP address of the destination host and TCP/IP will begin communicating with that host.

The screen capture below shows two packets. The first packet (frame 1) is Sally's name resolution request being sent to the WINS server. The packet is not broadcast; it goes directly to the WINS server. The second packet (frame 2), which is expanded, shows the WINS server responding to Sally with the IP address for the NetBIOS name Harry.

If the NetBIOS name is not in the WINS database, the server sends a response to the originator of the request stating that the NetBIOS name is not registered. This is a negative name query response. When a negative name query response is returned to the originator of the name query, that host will continue with the next method of NetBIOS name resolution, which is to broadcast for name resolution.

In the conference room analogy, whenever someone wants to talk to someone else, they simply call the registrar. When Sally wants to talk to Harry, she calls the registrar. The registrar is able to look at the most current listing of attendees and give either a positive or negative response. In a positive response, the registrar returns the name and number to the originator of the name query. Sally can now contact Harry. If the registrar returns a negative response, which means that she does not have an entry for Harry, Sally will politely say thank you to the registrar, hang up the phone, and then broadcast for Harry. As long as the database is current, the registrar will be able to resolve most queries.

The following illustration shows Sally asking the registrar for Harry's number, in the same way that a host on the network will send a query to the WINS server to get NetBIOS name resolution to another host.

Rita, what is Harry's number?

Sally

Now imagine that instead of just a couple of people at the conference, there are 1,000. This means there are 1,000 registrations and 1,000 people using the database for resolution. The chore of being the registrar could be overwhelming as the number of attendees grows. Doing both registrations and resolutions would be exhausting.

On a network, the WINS service consumes resources on the server on which it's installed. The number of WINS clients and the number of NetBIOS applications determines the overall draw on the server. It is estimated that one WINS server can service 10,000 clients. Although only one WINS server is necessary, it is recommended that a second WINS server be used for fault tolerance and redundancy. In any case, an administrator has to closely monitor the NetBIOS name resolution drain on the server resources. WINS servers can also be configured to share databases in a large internetwork.

Because WINS clients send registration and resolution requests directly to a WINS server, one WINS server can service many subnets. The name registrations and requests are not broadcast, so they will go through routers to the WINS server.

When a WINS client is properly shut down, the client sends a name release request to the WINS server. This lets the WINS server know that that NetBIOS name is no longer in use by that host. The WINS server marks that entry in the database as no longer in use. Now, when another host wants to register that NetBIOS name, the WINS server knows that it is available.

WINS Manager

To administer the WINS database, an administrator uses the WINS Manager utility. On a Windows NT server, the WINS service must be installed and the hosts configured to register with the WINS server. The WINS Manager is located by clicking Start ➢ Programs ➢ Administrative Tools ➢ WINS Manager.

Below is a screen capture of the WINS Manager utility. The entries in this WINS database include several NetBIOS names and IP addresses. This database will be used for resolution when any host that is configured to use it requests resolution. Some of the NetBIOS names that you may recognize include a few entries for Sally and the NT domain named Jumpstart.

static entry

A manual entry in the WINS database that is made by the administrator for a non-WINS client.

The entries include the NetBIOS name of the host, the IP address of the host, the expiration date, and the time of the entry. Another column shows the version of each entry. This hexadecimal version number starts at 1 and continues to increment as each entry is entered or updated. This is how the WINS service knows the most recent changes to the database. Every service that each NetBIOS host is registering must have a particular entry in the database; that is why there are multiple entries for each NetBIOS name.

On an internetwork that has non-WINS clients, an administrator may decide to manually enter the name of each non-WINS client into the WINS database. This is called a **static entry**. The benefit of configuring a static entry in the WINS database is that no host that registers with this WINS database can use the statically configured name. An additional benefit is that all the WINS clients can now get resolution to the non-WINS host.

To configure a static entry in WINS, enter the WINS Manager, click the Mappings menu, and choose Static Mappings, as shown below.

Click the Add Mappings button, then fill in the dialog box and click Add to complete adding an entry. In the Type field, you can specify the type of service that the non-WINS client is configured for and needs to have entered in the WINS database. In the screen capture below, a static mapping has been configured for the Administration server.

Now that the mapping has been configured, WINS will not let any WINS clients register with the name of ADMIN_SRV. If any WINS clients try to get resolution to ADMIN_SRV, the WINS database will be able to provide that resolution.

WINS provides an excellent service for automatically registering NetBIOS names and performing NetBIOS name resolution. Many networks today use WINS and a responsibility of many network administrators is to maintain WINS.

Review Questions

Terms to Know
- ❏ workstation service
- ❏ server service
- ❏ negative acknowledgment
- ❏ NetBIOS name cache
- ❏ NetBIOS name query
- ❏ network bandwidth
- ❏ NetBIOS name server
- ❏ static entry

1. What does WINS stand for?

_____

2. Without WINS, how does name registration take place?

_____

3. List two NetBIOS services.

_____

_____

4. If WINS receives a NetBIOS name registration, and that name has already been registered, describe what the WINS server does.

_____

5. When a workstation not using WINS powers down, is a name release packet broadcast?

_____

6. When a workstation using WINS powers down, is a name release packet sent to the WINS server?

_____

7. If a WINS server replies to a host with a negative acknowledgment, what does the host do next?

_____

8. Where is the first place that TCP/IP looks to resolve a NetBIOS name?

_____

9. Describe what a WINS server does when a registration comes in and there is already an entry for the NetBIOS name in the database.

_____

10. How does a TCP/IP host know where to find a WINS server?

_____

Chapter

12

IP version 6

Throughout this book, you have looked at TCP/IP addresses used with Internet Protocol version 4. Because of the enormous growth of the Internet and other factors that you will learn about in this chapter, IP version 4 is going to be replaced by IP version 6.

Most of the principles that you learned in this book apply to IPv6; some have been updated and some replaced. It will be useful in working with IPv6 to have a good foundational knowledge of IPv4.

In this chapter you will learn about:

 The need for a new version of IP

 IPv6's form of addressing

 Plans for the proposed transition from IPv4 to IPv6

The Need for a New Version of TCP/IP

Internet Protocol version 4 (IPv4)
The current version of IP that has been in use for over 20 years.

Internet Protocol version 6 (IPv6)
The formal name of the new version of IP that will be the new standard.

Internet Protocol, Next Generation (IPng)
The informal name of IPv6.

6BONE
The IPv6 backbone that is currently being used to build and test the IPv6 network infrastructure.

The Internet Protocol that is a standard today was created in the early 1970s. The current version is **Internet Protocol version 4 (IPv4)**. IPv4 has proven to be a stable and fully developed protocol; however, due to the enormous growth of the Internet, IPv4 is no longer viable. **Internet Protocol version 6 (IPv6)** will soon replace IPv4 as the Internet standard. IPv6 is also called **Internet Protocol, Next Generation (IPng)**.

IPng was proposed and recommended at an IETF meeting in July 1994 (in RFC 1752). The proposal to replace IPv4 as the Internet Protocol was accepted by the Internet Engineering Steering Group and IPng became a proposed standard. In August 1998, the proposed standard was upgraded to draft standard. Many RFCs have been written about IPv6 and are available on the Internet for further examination.

The Name of the New Protocol

The reason that we are going from IPv4 to IPv6 and not IPv5 is that a protocol named IPv5 already exists and is referred to in RFC 1946 as ST2 and ST2+. IPv5 is not a replacement for IPv4 and has very limited use.

The Next Generation references Star Trek, the Next Generation. This protocol suite will replace IPv4 just as the Next Generation crew replaced the old crew of the USS Enterprise.

IPng is not just an IPv4 upgrade; it is an overhauled protocol. Many of the features are similar, and the foundational methods of IPv4 are still the same. However, the addressing is different, and the headers are more specialized and lighter. IPv6 provides more options, including more flow control and enhanced security.

Since early 1998, a testing and pre-production network for IPv6 on the Internet has been online. This network, called **6BONE**, has grown to more than 400 sites and interconnecting networks in 40 countries. With the 6BONE network stabilizing, a transition to IPv6 will begin soon. The transition to a total IPv6 network is expected to take up to 10 years. Once implemented, IPv6 should be the standard for decades. The transition is described later in this chapter.

IPv6 Addressing

IPv4 is running out of network addresses, and routing tables are overflowing. In the early '90s, it was evident that something had to be done. Committees and teams were formed among many corporations and engineers. The result of the collaborative research and testing is IPv6. The design engineers have focused their improvements in the areas of addressing, efficiency, and enhanced security.

This section focuses on the addressing used in IPv6. The new protocol will provide many more IP addresses than the present version. And these new addresses will be written in hexadecimal form and will require a new type of notation.

IPv4 Addresses and IPv6 Addresses

In IPv4, there are 32 bits in every address. This means that there are approximately 4 billion unique IP addresses. This would have been enough addresses to support the original purpose of the ARPAnet. But as the ARPAnet grew into the Internet, and an enormous number of hosts connected to the network, IP addresses have been depleted.

IPv6 uses 128-bit addresses, which are exponentially larger than the address size of IPv4. Therefore, IPv6 supports a number of addresses that is 4 billion times the 4 billion addresses of the IPv4 address space. This works out to be:

IPv4 addresses (2^{32}):

4,294,967,296

IPv6 addresses (2^{128}):

340,282,366,920,938,463,463,374,607,431,768,211,456

This is an extremely large number of unique IP addresses. To put that number into an easier-to-comprehend concept, assume the Earth's surface is 511,263,971,197,990 square meters. Then, for every square meter of the surface of the Earth, there would be:

665,570,793,348,866,943,898,599

unique IP addresses.

Harry—The Next Generation

The following illustration shows Harry the Host in the IPv4 world as one of a few hosts; but with IPv6, Harry will be one of a huge number.

Harry   Harry

IPv4   IPv6

Why should we be able to use so many IP addresses? Did the designers go overboard? One plan proposed 64-bit addresses. But the designers of IPv6 determined that that might limit the growth of the network in the future.

Think of the future and the types of products that might need a unique IP address. It's possible to imagine that every item in your house will be connected to the Internet. You will be able to control air conditioning and heating through the Internet. Some other appliances that might be accessible to the Web include lighting, microwave ovens, refrigerators, automobile parts, cell phones, laptop computers, pagers, VCRs, and stereos. Because these appliances will be connected to the Internet, they will have a unique IP address.

Use your imagination to continue the list. Your Web-enabled refrigerator will be available to you and the manufacturer through the Web. Maybe you'll check the contents of the fridge through a Web browser before you leave work. Before you leave work, you'll access any item in your home over the Internet. You'll start dinner, adjust the temperature, and bring the car around to the front of the building. Is this possible? We'll see, but in any case, we'll have an addressing scheme that would provide enough addresses.

The New Hexadecimal IPv6 Addresses

In this book, you have looked at IPv4. These addresses are 32-bit addresses that look like this:

    192.168.2.100

IPv6 addresses are 128-bit addresses and are written in hexadecimal form. You will recall from Chapter 3 that the hexadecimal numbering system uses the same 0 to 9 digits as decimal, then uses A, B, C, D, E, and F to represent 10, 11, 12, 13, 14, and 15. The decimal 16 is represented in hexadecimal as 10. The address below is an example of an IPv6 address taken from RFCs 1884 and 1924, which describe IPv6 addressing and encoding:

    EFDC:BA62:7654:3201:EFDC:BA72:7654:3210

This is an example of the "full" IPv6 address wherein all 32 hex digits have a value that is significant. An IPv6 address with many 0s can be as short as eight hex digits. Because the IPv6 addresses are 128 bits in length, a new written standard has to be implemented. Using the IPv4 style of addresses, a 128-bit address would be represented by as many as 63 decimal numbers. Because that would be unreasonable, hexadecimal numbers are used to represent the binary addresses. Each section of hex characters represents 16 bits of the address. These 32 hex characters use seven colons as separators. This address is referred to as a 39-character address (32 + 7). Some addresses will have several 0s within the address. For example:

    1080:0000:0000:0000:0008:0800:200C:417A

To make notation of this address easier, the non-significant and leading 0s can be dropped. So the above address can be written as:

    1080:0:0:0:8:800:200C:417A

Even this shortened address seems too long. Fortunately, we can shorten it one more time. Because the address has several consecutive 0s, we can drop those and just push the colons together. The above address can be written using the **double-colon notation** method as:

    1080::8:800:200C:417A

Double-Colon Notation

Whenever you see an address that uses double-colon notation, it won't be instantly obvious how many and which 0s are missing. Expanding an address that uses the double-colon notation is a two-step process for humans. First, write eight *x*s separated by colons and replace the *x*s with values in the address that are to the left of the double-colon, moving from left to right. For example:

    1080:x:x:x:x:x:x:x

Then, starting from the furthest right side of the address, replace *x*s with values moving from right to left. For example:

    1080:x:x:x:x:x:x:417A

    1080:x:x:x:x:x:200C:417A

    1080:x:x:x:x:800:200C:417A

    1080:x:x:x:8:800:200C:417A

Now that the given values have been exhausted, replace each of the remaining *x*s with a 0.

    1080:0:0:0:8:800:200C:417A

TIP

An important rule in double-colon notation is that double colons can be used only once in an address.

An IPv4 address can be used within the IPv6 addressing scheme. The hexadecimal IPv4 address is placed in the last 32 bits of the IPv6 address. For example, the IPv4 address of

    192.168.2.100

within an IPv6 address is

    ::C0A8:0264

(which is using the double-colon notation for 0:0:0:0:0:0:C0A8:0264).

Converting decimal to hexadecimal is simply accomplished by using a calculator.

TEST IT OUT: CONVERTING IPV4 ADDRESSES TO IPV6 ADDRESSES

To convert an IPv4 to an IPv6 address, you first convert each section of the decimal address to hexadecimal. Then, because each hex value must be represented by two characters, you add a 0 to any values that have only one digit. Next, simply put the converted first and second octets together to form a four-character hex value. Finally, insert a colon and do the same for the converted third and fourth octet.

As an example, try converting 10.153.92.151 to an IPv6 address. The solution is:

1. Using a decimal to hex calculator, convert decimal 10 to hex:

   10 = A

2. Convert decimal 153 to hex:

   153 = 99

3. Convert decimal 92 to hex:

   92 = 5C

4. Convert decimal 151 to hex:

   151 = 97

5. Each of these hex values must be represented by two characters. Add a 0 to any values that have only one digit (A becomes 0A).

6. Put the hex digits together: 0A99:5C97

Now try this example: Convert 192.168.15.73 to an IPv6 address. The solution is as follows:

1. 192 = C0
2. 168 = A8
3. 15 = F
4. 73 = 49
5. F becomes 0F
6. Putting all the hex digits together, you have C0A8:0F49.

IPv6 Special Addresses

Many regulations apply to IPv6 addressing and many RFCs have been written about them. As the roll-out of IPv6 continues, many of these regulations will become common practice for administrators. Below are a couple of the more interesting regulations regarding special addressing concerns of IPv6.

The Unspecified Address

The address 0:0:0:0:0:0:0:0 is called the unspecified address. It must never be assigned to any host. It indicates the absence of an address. An unspecified address is used, for example, when an IPv6 host sends a packet seeking an address. The source address portion of the packet will contain the unspecified address. This is similar to a host sending a DHCP packet trying to discover an address.

The Loopback Address

The loopback address in IPv6 is 0:0:0:0:0:0:0:1. A host uses this address to send an IPv6 packet to itself. It can never be assigned to any host. This is similar to the IPv4 address of 127.0.0.1. Administrators use this address to aid in troubleshooting TCP/IP issues. As discussed earlier, an administrator can ping the loopback address to confirm that TCP/IP is bound correctly to the network card.

IPv6 Documentation

Many corporations and individuals are diligently working on the transition to IPv6. More than 180 RFCs have been published that reference this new standard. These RFCs cover everything from the inception of IPv6 to the transition plans. They include issues about addressing, header information, routing, and the organizations that will monitor IPv6.

These RFCs can be located by accessing the companion Web site for this book, which is referenced in Appendix D. In the next decade, network administrators will be called upon to aid in the transition to IPv6. The administrators who begin working with IPv6 soon will be in the greatest demand mid-transition. Therefore, it is important that network administrators get a handle on IPv6 as soon as possible. Training and hands-on experience will be invaluable. Several Web sites have been set up to involve volunteers with the IPv4 to IPv6 transition.

Improvements of IPv6

You learned in an earlier section about the dramatic increase of potential addresses that IPv6 will offer. Some of the other key improvements in IPv6 include:

- ◆ Enhanced security (described in RFC 1827).
- ◆ New types of packet addressing with multicast and anycast addressing.
- ◆ New IPv6 RFCs for protocols that have been discussed in this book, including DHCP, DNS, ICMP, IP, TCP and UDP. With the new IPv6 headers being streamlined, these other TCP/IP protocols have been improved.

Some redundant IPv4 header fields have been eliminated or made optional. The amount of resources used by every host and router to process a packet is reduced, which increases the amount of available bandwidth. Even though the IPv6 address is four times larger than an IPv4 address, the IPv6 headers are only twice as large. This means that packets are "slicker" and tighter without much extra, useless padding to slow them down.

Packets in IPv6 can have labels indicating that they belong to a certain flow, or group, of packets. Therefore, as the flow of packets moves through a router, the routers can keep certain similar packet types moving together, while other packets with a lower priority wait. This gives the sender the possibility of a **real-time** service. Such services include video conferencing and other communications that need to move through the Internet with the highest priority for almost immediate or real-time reception.

IPv6 describes rules for three types of addressing:

Unicast   One host to one other host. This is similar to much of the addressing that you have looked at in this book.

Anycast   One host to the nearest of multiple hosts. This type of address is used to send a packet to a group of hosts, but only the nearest host processes the packet. The idea is that the host that receives the packet can relay the information to the other hosts in the group. This type of addressing did not exist with IPv4.

Multicast   One host to multiple hosts. This type of address is similar to the multicast that you learned about in this book.

An IPv6 packet contains options that are specified as part of the header that is examined only at the destination, thus speeding up overall network performance.

real-time
A type of data that is available instantaneously. The term usually refers to video or audio conferencing.

unicast
A packet that is sent from one host to one other host.

anycast
A packet that is sent from one host to the nearest host within a group of hosts.

multicast
A packet that is sent from one host to many other hosts at the same time.

235

The Transition Plan to IPv6

RFC 1933 describes a plan to transition the existing IPv4 Internet to the new IPv6 Internet. A major consideration is how to convert the Internet into IPv6 without disrupting the operation of the existing IPv4 network. This proposal has a nickname of **SIT (Simple IPv6 Transition)**.

Simple IPv6 Transition (SIT)
The proposed plan to transition to IPv6.

The transition plan includes two phases. The first phase includes upgrading several components to the IPv6 level so that at the end of phase 1, there will be a combination of both IPv4 and IPv6 hosts and routers on the Internet. In the second phase of the transition, the remaining IPv4 addresses and components will be replaced, so that by the end of phase 2, there will be only IPv6 hosts and routers.

Some of the key objectives that SIT must comply with are detailed in the Simple IPv6 Transition proposal. These include:

◆ IPv6 and IPv4 hosts can coexist on the Internet during the transition. There will be no "cut-over" date, so IPv4 hosts can continue to operate on the IPv6 network.

◆ IPv6 routers and hosts can be deployed across the Internet in an independent fashion. Existing IPv4 hosts and routers may be upgraded to IPv6 at any time without being dependent on any other hosts or routers being upgraded.

◆ The transition will be as easy as possible for end-users, system administrators, and network operators to understand and carry out. As existing IPv4 hosts or routers are upgraded to IPv6, they will continue to use their existing addresses in the IPv6 form.

◆ IPv6 will have minimal upgrade dependencies. DNS servers will be the first component to be upgraded to handle IPv6 addresses. There are no prerequisites to upgrading routers.

◆ IPv6 will have low start-up costs. Budget considerations are always an issue. There must be little or no preparation work to upgrade existing IPv4 systems to IPv6, or to deploy new IPv6 systems.

The following illustration shows the upgraded protocol. Harry is working in a leaner, meaner, and more efficient network. Data transfer is faster, and security is enhanced.

Review Questions

Terms to Know
❑ IPv4
❑ IPv6
❑ IPng
❑ 6BONE
❑ double-colon
  notation
❑ real-time
❑ unicast
❑ anycast
❑ multicast
❑ SIT

1. IPv4 uses _____ bit addresses.

2. IPv6 uses _____ bit addresses.

3. Write the following IPv6 address with the least amount of characters:
   109A:3210:0:0:0:0:0213:412B

   _____

4. Convert the following IPv4 address to an IPv6 address: 10.25.135.123

   _____

5. Convert the following IPv4 address to an IPv6 address: 192.168.31.4

   _____

6. Expand the following IPv6 address to display all 39 characters (colons
   count as a character) that are compressed with the double-colon notation:
   A013:1234:34::8:411A

   _____

7. List two reasons why a new protocol is needed.

   _____

8. What is the name of the proposed plan to transition IPv6?

   _____

9. Describe the phases of the IPv6 transition plan.

   _____

Appendix
A

Answers to
Review Questions

Chapter 1

1. ARPAnet

2. Any three of the following: No one point can be more critical than any other; it needs on-the-fly rerouting of data; it needs redundant routes to any destination; it can connect different types of computers over different types of networks; it cannot be controlled by a single corporation.

3. Host

4. A packet-switched network sends packets of data across the network independent of one another; each of the packets takes its own route. A circuit-switched network uses the same path, or circuit, for all data.

5. Request For Comment, a paper thoroughly describing a new protocol or technology

6. NCP

7. False—TCP/IP is a suite of protocols.

8. Internet Engineering Task Force, a governing body of the Internet

9. Any four of the following: It is a widely published, open standard; it is compatible with different computer systems; it works on different hardware and network configurations; it is a routable protocol; it has reliable, efficient data delivery; it has a single addressing scheme.

10. 1983

Chapter 2

1. A protocol is a set of rules for communicating that the sending and receiving hosts use when they send data back and forth.

2. A packet is a unit of data that is sent from an originating host to a destination host on a network.

3. The OSI model was created to break down the many tasks involved in moving data from one host to another.

4. Application, Presentation, Session, Transport, Network, Data-Link, and Physical

5. Application, Transport, Internet, and Network Interface

6. IPX/SPX, TCP/IP, AppleTalk

7. Packets

8. Headers

9. Data-Link

10. LLC (Logical Link Control) and MAC (Media Access Control)

Chapter 3

1. Any three of the following: MAC, Ethernet, physical, or NIC

2. FF:FF:FF:FF:FF:FF

3. IP, ARP, ICMP, IGMP

4. Logical addressing and routing

5. ARP

6. Two minutes and up to ten minutes if used again

7. Broadcast, FF:FF:FF:FF:FF:FF

8. The hardware address of the host that sent the ARP request

9. Ping

10. Source IP address, source hardware address, destination IP address, and destination hardware address (set to FF:FF:FF:FF:FF:FF)

11. Source IP address, source hardware address, destination IP address, and destination hardware address

12. Ethernet
    Token Ring
    FDDI

13. The manufacturer "burns in" the address to a chip on the card when the card is manufactured.

14. 12 hexadecimal characters

Chapter 4

1. TCP (Transmission Control Protocol) and UDP (User Datagram Protocol)

2. TCP: Connection-oriented and guaranteed

   UDP: Connectionless and not guaranteed

3. Three-way handshake

4. An acknowledgment

5. UDP does not wait for acknowledgments.

6. The application

7. UDP can transfer data faster.

8. TCP guarantees delivery of data.

9. 761

10. 768

11. TCP

12. It verifies that the packet was received correctly.

Chapter 5

1. At ports

2. 65,536

3. 1–1024

4. An FTP client logs into the FTP server and requests files by using TCP/IP. The FTP server sends the requested files back to the client by using TCP/IP.

5. An HTTP client sends a request to an HTTP server by using TCP/IP. The HTTP server sends the requested files back to the client by using TCP/IP, and the files are displayed with a Web browser application.

6. SNMP, Telnet, SMTP, and TFTP

1a. 195

1b. 165

1c. 155

1d. 231

7. A host can send packets only to the gateway, and the gateway then has the responsibility of sending the packets on to their destination.

8. Yes, a server can be running several services and listening at different ports for requests.

9. The standard for HTTP requests is port 80. To "hide" a Web site, an administrator can set the Web server to listen to any other port where standard requests are not made (the administrator can set it to listen only to port 8080 or port 8090, for example). In this way, only someone who knows that the Web server is listening at the hidden port can access the Web server.

10. Internet Assigned Number Authority (IANA)

11. 80

12. IP address
Transport layer protocol (TCP or UDP)
port number

13. A nice looking, easy-to-use application used to access an FTP server.

Chapter 6

1a. 195

1b. 165

1c. 155

1d. 231

2a. 0000 1010

2b. 0011 1001

2c. 0111 1111

2d. 1111 1111

3a. 1–127

3b. 128–191

3c. 192–223

4. A Class D address is used for multicasting. A Class D address is illegal as a host IP address, but is used for sending data to several hosts at the same time.

5. 254

6. 16,384

7. 16,777,214

8. An IP broadcast address

9. The network address

10. A host cannot have an address of all 0s or all 1s; such an address is always invalid.

11. $2^N - 2$

Chapter 7

1. Manually and automatically

2. Discover, offer, request, and acknowledgment

3. All four

4. Hardware address of the client

5. Server address, offered IP address, client hardware address

6. To reserve an IP address for a particular hardware address. That host will always get the same IP address.

7. Most of the time. Only in a few situations—for example, when only a few hosts are on a network—should the administrator use manually configured addresses.

8. After 50 percent of the lease has expired

9. The DHCP client's hardware address is included in the offer.

10. Servers, printers, routers

Chapter 8

1a. 255.255.255.192

1b. 150.150.0.64, 150.150.0.128, 150.150.0.192

1c. 150.150.0.65–150.150.0.126

150.150.0.129–150.150.0.190

150.150.0.193–150.150.0.254

1d. Network: 150.150.255.128
Range of IP addresses: 150.150.255.129–150.150.255.190

1e. 1,022

1f. 62

2a. 255.255.255.128

2b. 151.151.0.128, 151.151.1.0, 151.151.1.128

2c. 151.15.10.129–151.151.0.254
151.151.1.1–151.151.1.126
151.151.1.129–151.151.1.254

2d. Network: 151.151.255.0
Range of IP addresses: 151.151.255.1–151.151.255.126

2e. 510

2f. 126

3a. 255.255.255.0

3b. 152.152.1.0, 152.152.2.0, 152.152.3.0

3c. 152.152.1.1–152.152.1.254
152.152.2.1–152.152.2.254
152.152.3.1–152.152.3.254

3d. Network: 152.152.254.0
Range of IP addresses: 152.152.254.1–152.152.254.254

3e. 254

3f. 254

4a. 255.255.255.240

4b. 200.200.200.16, 200.200.200.32, 200.200.200.48

4c. 200.200.200.17–200.200.200.30
200.200.200.33–200.200.200.47
200.200.200.49–200.200.200.62

4d. Network: 200.200.200.224
Range of IP addresses: 200.200.200.225–200.200.200.238

4e. 14

4f. 14

5a. 255.255.255.224

5b. 201.201.201.32, 201.201.201.64, 201.201.201.96

5c. 201.201.201.33–201.201.201.62
201.201.201.65–201.201.201.94
201.201.201.97–201.201.201.126

5d. Network: 201.201.201.192

5e. 6

5f. 30

6. Trick question—the address is invalid.

7. 255.255.255.192

8. 255.255.252.0

9. 255.255.254.0

10. 255.255.128.0

11a. 254

11b. 65,534

Chapter 9

1. Host name resolution and NetBIOS name resolution

2. Local host, HOSTS file, DNS, NetBIOS name cache, WINS, broadcast, LMHOSTS file

3. NetBIOS name cache, WINS, Broadcast, LMHOSTS file, HOSTS file, DNS

4. The IP address needs to be on the left.

5. Put an entry in the HOSTS file for www.sybex.com.

6. Add #PRE to the ACCT_SRV entry in the LMHOSTS file to have the name and IP address of ACCT_SRV always in NetBIOS name cache.

7. \SYSTEMROOT\SYSTEM32\DRIVERS\ETC

8. No, only NetBIOS names can be in the file.

9. The #PRE switch and the LMHOSTS file are used.

10. nbtstat –R

11. Host name resolution

12. Host name resolution

13. NetBIOS name resolution

14. HOSTNAME

Chapter 10

1. HOSTS.TXT

2. RFCs 1034 and 1035

3. A period

4. A resolver

5. IP address configuration has the address of the DNS server.

6. A recursive query

7. An iterative query

8. Primary, secondary, and caching-only

9. Zone transfer

10. Yes

11. No, caching only servers do not have a copy of the database.

12. An A record

13. Inverse or reverse lookup

Chapter 11

1. Windows Internet Naming Service

2. Broadcast

3. Workstation service and server service

4. The WINS server sends three challenges to the IP address of the NetBIOS name currently registered. If there is a response, the WINS server sends a negative acknowledgment to the newcomer; if there is no response to the challenge, the database is updated and a positive response is sent to the newcomer.

5. No

6. Yes

7. Broadcast

8. NetBIOS name cache

9. WINS sends a series of three "challenges" to the currently registered IP address. If there is a response, the new host cannot have that name. If there is no response, the new host can have the name.

10. The IP address of the WINS server is an optional parameter of the TCP/IP configuration.

Chapter 12

1. 32

2. 128

3. 109A:3210::213:412B

4. ::0A15:877B

5. ::C0A8:1F04

6. A013:1234:0034:0000:0000:0000:0008:411A

7. More addresses, enhanced security, greater efficiency

8. SIT, Simple IPv6 Transition

9. There are two phases. The first phase will have IPv4 and IPv6 coexisting on the same network, and the second phase will eliminate all of IPv4.

10. 10 years

11. AC14:1910

12. 7F00:0001

Appendix B

Glossary

Numbers

$2^N - 2$ Equation used to figure out the number of subnets and hosts per subnet that can be created with a subnet mask. N is the number of bits that you are using for the subnet portion or the host portion of the address.

6BONE   The IPv6 backbone that is currently being used to build and test the IPv6 network infrastructure.

A

A record   Also called a Host record, it contains the names and IP addresses of hosts.

Acknowledgment   A packet sent by a host to confirm receipt of a packet. The sending host waits for an acknowledgment packet before sending additional data. The destination host sends acknowledgments as packets are received.

Address Resolution Protocol (ARP)   A protocol used to translate an IP address to a hardware address.

Alias   A simpler or alternative name for a host.

Anonymous   Account set up so that anyone can access files on an FTP server without a secret password.

Anycast   A packet that is sent from one host to the nearest host within a group of hosts.

Application layer   The top layer of the DoD and OSI models where applications listen for and respond to requests.

Application Programming Interface (API)   A common interface that enables programmers to write programs to a standard specification.

ARP cache   An area in RAM that holds recently performed IP-to-hardware address resolutions.

ARP reply   A packet that is returned to the sender of the ARP request and that includes the IP address and hardware address that was requested.

ARP request   A broadcast packet that seeks to resolve an IP address to a hardware address.

ARPAnet   The Advanced Research Projects Agency's supernetwork—the predecessor of the Internet.

ASCII text file   A file that is stored as text only—no fancy characters. It can be edited with any text editor such as Notepad or Edit.

B

Bandwidth   The amount of data that can move through the cabling.

Binary   The base-2 number system that computers use to represent data. It consists of only two digits: 0 and 1.

Binary format   A compressed file format.

Broadcast   When broadcasting to get name resolution, the host "hollers" the name to be resolved onto the network.

Broadcast packet   A packet that is addressed to all hosts; the broadcast address is a universal address enabling all hosts to receive the packet. Routers will generally stop broadcast packets from moving on to another network.

C

Cache   Temporary storage of information that is accessed quickly.

Caching-only server   A name server that does not have a copy of a DNS database.

Canonical Name (CNAME) record An alias or code name for a host that already has an A record.

Circuit-switched network A network on which all data in a communication takes the same path.

Classless Inter-Domain Routing (CIDR) An IP addressing scheme that uses a slash followed by a number to highlight the network portion of an address instead of using a subnet mask.

Connectionless Communication that occurs without a connection being set up first.

Connection-oriented A type of protocol in which a connection is established and maintained until the application programs at each end have exchanged their message or messages.

Contiguous bits One bit following another.

Custom subnet mask A non-standard subnet mask that a network administrator uses to make more efficient use of a network address by creating more subnets.

CuteFTP An easy-to-use FTP command interpreter application that turns your mouse clicks into FTP commands.

D

Decimal The base-10 number system that people use to represent data. It consists of 10 digits: 0, 1, 2, 3, 4, 5, 6, 7, 8, 9.

Default gateway A parameter included with the router's IP address that packets are sent to en route to a remote network.

Department of Defense (DoD) The branch of the United States military maintaining national defense.

DHCP acknowledgment (ack) The final step in using DHCP to lease a new IP address or to renew an IP address lease. A DHCP ack is broadcast for new IP address leases and sent directly to the DHCP client for renewals. The packet says, "It's a done deal! You can have this IP address, and here are some extra parameters that you can have."

DHCP discover The first step in using DHCP to lease an IP address. A DHCP discover packet is broadcast saying, "Hey, who is a DHCP server?"

DHCP offer The second step in using DHCP to lease an IP address. A DHCP offer packet is broadcast saying, "I'm a DHCP server; how would you like this fine address?"

DHCP request The third step in using DHCP to lease a new IP address and the first step in renewing an IP address lease. A DHCP request packet is broadcast for new IP address leases and sent directly to the DHCP server for renewals. The packet says, "Yes, I would like to have this IP address."

DHCP server A host running a service to lease IP addresses to other hosts. The DHCP server is configured by an administrator with the pool, or scope, of addresses to be leased.

Domain A unique portion of the name space in which an administrator creates an authoritative database of records to give resolution of names within the zone to an IP address.

Domain name space The entire inverted tree of Internet names.

Domain Name System (DNS) Distributed system used on the Internet to resolve host names to IP addresses.

Dotted decimal notation The decimal representation of an IP address or subnet mask. Four decimal numbers separated by periods (or dots) is the preferred way to represent an address or mask.

Double-colon notation   A shorthand method of writing IPv6 addresses without including non-significant 0s.

E

Encapsulation   The wrapping of a packet into the appropriate package or format.

Exclusion   An IP address that falls into a range of addresses to be leased, but that has been set by an administrator not to be leased.

F

Fault tolerance   Taking into account any failures.

File Transfer Protocol (FTP)   An application used to transfer files from one host to another and to store the files on the requesting host.

Firewall   An application that prevents certain types of data from passing from a public network to an internal, private network.

FTP command interpreter   A nice looking, easy-to-use application used to access an FTP server.

FTP command line utility   A non-mouse and non-fancy interface used to access an FTP server.

FTP server   Server on which an FTP server application is running to transfer files to clients.

FTP/TCP/IP   A packet that has an FTP header on top of a TCP header on top of an IP header.

G

Global option   A parameter that is set at the DHCP server and that applies to all scopes of IP addresses that this DHCP server serves.

H

Headers   Bits of information attached to each packet that usually include addressing and routing details; the information acts like a little sticky note on the packet.

Hexadecimal   A base-16 numbering system containing 16 sequential numbers (including 0) as base units before adding a new position for the next number; the hexadecimal system uses the numbers 0–9 and then the letters A–F.

Host   Any device (such as a workstation, server, mainframe, or printer) on a network or internetwork that has a TCP/IP address.

Host name resolution   The process of resolving a host name to an IP address.

HOSTNAME utility   A simple utility that determines the host name of the computer in which you are working.

HOSTS file   A file of host names and IP addresses.

hosts.txt   The original file that contained name-to-IP address relationships.

HTTP/TCP/IP   A packet with an HTTP header on top of a TCP header on top of an IP header.

Hyperlink   Underlined word on a Web site that links to another document on that Web server or possibly on another Web server.

Hypertext Markup Language (HTML)
The file format of Web pages housed on a Web server that can be displayed in a useful format by a Web browser.

Hypertext Transfer Protocol (HTTP)   An application used to transfer files from one host to another and to display the files at the requesting host.

I

IN-ADDR.ARPA Inverse address from the ARPAnet; a zone used to keep PTR records.

International Standards Organization (ISO) The organization that ratified the OSI model.

Internet Assigned Numbers Authority (IANA) An organization responsible for overseeing several aspects of the Internet.

Internet Engineering Task Force (IETF) A governing body of the Internet

Internet layer Layer between the Network Interface and Transport layers of the DoD model; protocols at the Internet layer focus on addressing.

Internet Protocol version 4 (IPv4) The current version of IP that has been in use for over 20 years.

Internet Protocol version 6 (IPv6) The formal name of the new version of IP that will become the standard.

Internet Protocol, Next Generation (IPng) The informal name of IPv6.

Internetwork Several smaller networks connected together.

IP address An address that IP uses to identify a unique network and host.

Iterative query A question asked with the expectation that the best information available will be returned so that more queries can be sent based that information.

L

LAN Manager A networking product that was the predecessor of Microsoft's Windows NT.

Layer A portion of the OSI model that is used to categorize specific concerns.

LMHOSTS file A file containing NetBIOS names and IP addresses that is used for name resolution.

Load balancing Spreading the workload across servers.

Local host A step in name resolution wherein a host examines its TCP/IP configuration to see whether the name being resolved is its own.

Local network Hosts that are on the same side of a router are considered on the same local network. Two hosts on the same local network have the exact same bit values in the network portion of their IP addresses.

Logical address This address can be modified; it refers only to the host.

Loopback An address that is used for diagnostic purposes, to test the TCP/IP stack of a TCP/IP host.

M

Mail eXchanger (MX) record A record that contains the address of the mail server.

Master DNS database The authoritative DNS database containing DNS records. The administrator can modify records in this database.

Microsoft TCP/IP client Any TCP/IP host that has installed and configured Microsoft's TCP/IP client software. This accounts for most TCP/IP hosts.

Multicast A packet that is sent from one host to many other hosts at the same time.

Multicast address A reserved IP address that Internet Group Management Protocol (IGMP) uses for streaming data. No one host can have this address, but several can receive data by listening to it.

N

Name resolution   The process of finding the IP address for the name of a computer.

Name server   A server running the DNS service that can provide name resolution.

Name Server (NS) record   A record that lists the IP address of a name server.

nbtstat   A utility used to monitor the names that are in NetBIOS name cache.

Negative acknowledgment   An acknowledgment sent from a host or server that says, "I received your request and the answer is no."

NetBIOS   Network Basic Input Output System; a program that enables applications on different computers to communicate within a local area network.

NetBIOS name cache   Temporary cache storage for NetBIOS names and IP addresses that have been resolved. The names and addresses are stored in RAM for rapid resolution.

NetBIOS name query   A packet asking for the IP address of a host with a particular NetBIOS name.

NetBIOS name resolution   The process of resolving a NetBIOS name to an IP address.

NetBIOS name server   A server that registers and resolves NetBIOS names.

NetBIOS names   The name given to a computer that is running a Microsoft operating system.

Network Address Translation (NAT)   An application that translates the IP address of the sending host to another IP address while relaying the TCP/IP data to another network.

Network administrator   A person who installs, monitors, and troubleshoots a network.

Network bandwidth   The amount of data that can be put onto a network based on other communication traffic already using the wire.

Network Control Protocol (NCP)   The protocol used before TCP/IP.

Network interface card (NIC)   A piece of hardware that is used to connect a host to a network; every host must have one in order to connect to a network.

Network Interface layer   Lowest layer of the DoD model, it acts as a host's connection, or interface, to the network.

Network topology   Describes how a network is connected and how each host knows when and how to transmit and receive data.

O

Octet   Eight bits of data.

Open Standards Interconnection (OSI) model   A seven-layer model used to break down the many tasks involved in moving data from one host to another.

P

Packet   A unit of data that is prepared for transmission onto a network.

Packet-switched network   A network on which the data in a communication takes several paths.

Parsing   Reading through a file looking for specific data.

Peer-layer communication   A type of communication in which each layer of the sending host communicates with the same layer of the receiving host.

Ping Packet InterNet Groper; a software utility that tests connectivity between two TCP/IP hosts.

Pointer (PTR) record A record that aids with IP address-to-host-name resolution.

Ports Numbered addresses where requests are sent and where applications listen for requests. Ports are numbered 1–65,536.

Primary name server The name server that holds the master DNS database.

Protocol stack Protocols that send and receive data.

Protocol suite A combination of protocols.

Protocols Rules or standards that govern communications between hosts.

Proxy server An application that relays TCP/IP traffic from one network to another while changing the IP address of the sending host.

R

Read/write A file that can be read from and written to.

Read-only A file that can be read but cannot be modified.

Real-time A type of data that is available instantaneously. The term usually refers to video or audio conferencing.

Records The information in the DNS database.

Recursive query A question asked with the expectation that the response will be either the complete answer or an error, nothing less.

Remote network A network other than the one that the host is on; a remote network is on the other side of a router. Two hosts on remote networks have different bit values in the network portion of their IP addresses.

Request For Comment (RFC) A paper thoroughly describing a new protocol or technology.

Reserved IP address An IP address that cannot be used as a valid host address.

Resolve To translate a logical to a physical address.

Resolver A client that is trying to resolve a host name to an IP address.

Root name servers Powerful name servers that contain addresses of the top-level name servers.

Router A host that interfaces with other networks and can move packets from one network to another.

Routing The process of determining which is the next path to send a packet so that it gets to its destination.

Routing table A table that contains the addresses indicating the best routes to other networks.

S

Scope A pool of IP addresses that a DHCP server leases to DHCP clients.

Scope option A parameter that is set at the DHCP server that applies to only one scope of IP addresses.

Secondary name server A name server that has a copy of the master DNS database.

Sequence numbers Numbers in a header that indicate the order of packets. If packets get out of order en route to the destination host, this numbering system enables packets to be rearranged in order at the destination host.

Server service A NetBIOS service that performs server activities such as file sharing.

Shares   A feature of several operating systems that is used to designate local resources that will be accessible across the network.

Simple IPv6 Transition (SIT)   The proposed plan to transition to IPv6.

Socket   IP address : TCP or UDP : port number.

Source-quench   An ICMP packet that is sent to slow down the transmission at the source.

Standard subnet mask   Also called a default subnet mask. For Class A = 255.0.0.0, for Class B = 255.255.0.0, and for Class C = 255.255.255.0.

Stanford Research Institute Network Information Center (SRI-NIC)   The site of early Internet growth and host-name maintenance.

Start Of Authority (SOA) record   The first record in a DNS database; it describes the database.

Static entry   A manual entry in the WINS database that is made by the administrator for a non-WINS client.

Stream   A series of packets sent without waiting for acknowledgments.

Subnet   A smaller network created by dividing a larger network.

Subnet bits   Bits used in the subnet mask to extend the number of bits available for the network portion of the IP address.

Subnet calculator   A software calculator that figures out subnet masks, valid networks, number of hosts, and host ranges. Several are available for download on the Internet.

Subnet goggles   A fictional set of goggles that IP wears when looking at an IP address to determine whether an address is local or remote.

Subnet mask   A parameter included with every IP address that highlights the network portion of the IP address.

Switch   A character or set of characters used to further enhance a command.

T

Three-way handshake   A three-step conversation initiated by TCP to set up a connection between hosts.

Time To Live (TTL)   The amount of time that the lease on an IP address is valid.

Transmission Control Protocol (TCP)   Protocol at the Transport layer that is connection oriented and guarantees delivery of packets. TCP is responsible for ensuring that a message is divided into the packets that IP manages and for reassembling the packets into the complete message at the other end.

Transmission Control Protocol/Internet Protocol (TCP/IP)   The suite of protocols that when combined create the "language of the Internet."

U

Unicast   A packet that is sent from one host to one other host.

Uniform Resource Locator (URL)   The address of a Web site that a user can surf to.

User Datagram Protocol (UDP)   A protocol offering a limited amount of service when messages are exchanged between hosts. No connection is set up and no acknowledgments are expected.

W

WAN connection　A connection between two LANs (local area networks) is a WAN (wide area network) connection.

Web browser application　A client application used for surfing the Web. Examples are Netscape Navigator and Microsoft Internet Explorer.

Web server　Server on which an HTTP server application is running; users can surf to this server and request that files be transferred and displayed.

Well-known ports　Port numbers 1–1,024, which are reserved for certain applications.

Windows Internet Naming Service (WINS)　Microsoft's NetBIOS name server that keeps NetBIOS names and IP addresses in a database and later gives name resolution.

Workstation service　A NetBIOS service that performs workstation activities such as using the local operating system.

Z

Zone transfer　The sending of a DNS database from one name server to another.

Appendix C

Acronym Expansion Guide

Acronym	What It Stands For
ack	acknowledgment
API	Application Programming Interface
ARP	Address Resolution Protocol
ARPA	Advanced Research Projects Agency
ARPAnet	Advanced Research Projects Agency Network
ASCII	American Standard Code for Information Interchange
BIND	Berkeley Internet Name Domain
bit	Binary digit
CNAME	Canonical name
DHCP	Dynamic Host Configuration Protocol
DNS	Domain Name System
DoD	Department of Defense
FDDI	Fiber Distributed Data Interface
FTP	File Transfer Protocol
HTML	Hypertext Markup Language
HTTP	Hypertext Transfer Protocol
IANA	Internet Assigned Numbers Authority
ICMP	Internet Control Message Protocol
IETF	Internet Engineering Task Force
IGMP	Internet Group Management Protocol
IP	Internet Protocol
IPng	Internet Protocol, Next Generation
IPv4	Internet Protocol version 4
IPv6	Internet Protocol version 6
IPX/SPX	Internetwork Packet Exchange/Sequenced Packet Exchange
ISO	International Organization for Standardization
ISP	Internet Service Provider
LAN	local area network

Acronym Expansion Guide

Acronym	What It Stands For
LLC	Logical Link Control
LMHOSTS	LAN Manager Hosts
MAC	Media Access Control
MX	Mail eXchanger
nak	negative acknowledgment
NCP	Network Control Protocol
NetBIOS	Network Basic Input Output System
NIC	Network Interface Card
NS	name server
OSI	Open Systems Interconnection
Ping	Packet InterNet Groper
RAM	Random Access Memory
RFC	Request For Comment
SIT	Simple IPv6 Transition
SMTP	Simple Mail Transfer Protocol
SNM	subnet mask
SNMP	Simple Network Management Protocol
SOA	Start Of Authority
SRI-NIC	Stanford Research Institute Network Information Center
TCP	Transmission Control Protocol
TCP/IP	Transmission Control Protocol/Internet Protocol
TFTP	Trivial File Transfer Protocol
TTL	Time To Live
UDP	User Datagram Protocol
URL	Uniform Resource Locator
WAN	wide area network
WINS	Windows Internet Naming Service
WWW	World Wide Web

Appendix D

What's on the Web Site

So much has been written about TCP/IP that to include all the relevant documentation in one book would be impossible. A *TCP/IP JumpStart* Web site has been set up to give you quick and current references to documents that have been discussed in this book, as well as to other Web sites of interest.

How to Access the *TCP/IP JumpStart* Companion Web Site

To access the *TCP/IP JumpStart* companion Web site:

1. Open a Web browser window and go to the Sybex Web site (http://www.sybex.com).
2. Scroll to the Search the Sybex Catalog area.
3. Type **2644**, which is the ISBN number of this book, or type **TCP/IP JumpStart**.
4. From the *TCP/IP JumpStart* book page on the Web site, click the Links button.

What You'll Find on the Web Site

The *TCP/IP JumpStart* Web site serves as a current reference to many materials that a TCP/IP administrator would need to access. Your exploration of TCP/IP documentation, tools, and utilities on the Internet can start at the *TCP/IP JumpStart* Web site. The Web site is updated regularly and includes links to information described in the following sections.

Requests For Comments

Throughout the book, I make many references to Requests For Comments. Many times, as an administrator or programmer, you will want to refer to the original or latest RFC to get more detailed information about a protocol. If you have never read an RFC, you're in for a treat. The *TCP/IP JumpStart* Web site has links to all RFCs that have been published.

Subnet Calculators

Administrators need to be able to determine the proper subnet, valid network, and correct host addresses based on the number of hosts and the number of networks that they work with. In this book, you were taught how to manually determine this information. To double-check your work, or maybe just to make it easier, the Web site has links to several subnet calculators.

Further Reading on IP Version 6

In Chapter 12 of this book, you learned about the next version of TCP/IP. IP version 6 is currently being tested and deployed, and the links on the companion Web site provide valuable, current information about this protocol.

Many of the linked Web sites have interesting articles about the history and growth of the Internet. Some sites include cool tools, such as one for tracing your route around the Internet.

Index

Symbols & Numbers

#PRE switch, 183
$2^N - 2$, 252
6BONE, 228, 252

A

A record, 206, 252
acknowledgment, 252
negative, 119, 213, 218, 256
of received packets, 26, 56, 58
acronyms, 262–263
Address Resolution Protocol (ARP), 42,
43–46, 252
addressing information in packet
header, 20
addressing scheme in TCP/IP, 12
Advanced Research Projects Agency, 4
alias, 252
in HOSTS file, 175
anonymous, 252
anonymous user, for FTP, 71
Anycast, 235, 252
API (Application Programming Interface),
168, 252
AppleTalk, 19
Application layer, 29, 252
basics, 68
ports and sockets, **68–70**
responsibilities of, **25**

Application Programming Interface (API),
168, 252
applications, termination at end of DHCP
lease, 119
ARP (Address Resolution Protocol), 42,
43–46, 252
broadcast for address resolution,
44–45
ARP cache, 43, 252
additions to, 45
ARP packets, **46**, *46*
ARP reply, 45, *46*, 252
ARP request broadcast, 43, 252
ARPAnet, **4–5**, 252
military requirements for, 5
ASCII text file, 252
for HOSTS file, 174
for LMHOSTS file, 182
assigning IP addresses, **102–109**
audio, sending streaming with IGMP,
50–51

B

bandwidth, 252, 256
broadcasting and, 181, 216
Berkeley Internet Name Domain (BIND),
202
binary digit, 83
binary file format, 71, 252

binary numbering system, 36, 80, 252
    converting decimal to, **84–89**
        using bit value method, **84–85**
        using calculator, **88–89**
        using division method, **86–87**
    converting to decimal, **83**
    reviewing, **82**
BIND (Berkeley Internet Name Domain), 202
bit value method, for decimal to binary conversion, **84–85**
bits, 83
    contiguous, 142, 253
boot process, loading entries in NetBIOS name cache, 183
broadcast, 252
    for name resolution, **180–181**, 188, 216
    to resolve hardware address, **44–45**
broadcast IP address, 93, 137
broadcast packets, 37, 252

C

cache, 198, 252
    ARP, 43, 252
        additions to, 45
    NetBIOS name, **177–178**, *184*, 214, 256
        displaying contents, **184–185**
        in host name resolution cycle, 188
        loading entries during boot process, 183
caching-only server, **205**, 252
calculator
    for decimal to binary conversion, **88–89**
    IP Subnet, *135*, 135
    subnet, 138
Canonical name record, 206, 253

Cerf, Vint, 7
checksum, in UDP header, 61
CIDR (Classless Inter-Domain Routing), 96, 253
circuit-switched network, 253
    moving data on, **9**, *9*
classes for IP addresses, **92–96**
    Class A, **92–93**
        custom subnet mask, **148–149**
        standard subnet mask for, 132
    Class B, **94**
        custom subnet mask, **150–151**
        standard subnet mask for, 132
    Class C, **95**
        custom subnet mask, **154–155**
        standard subnet mask for, 132
        valid hosts for, **152–155**
    Class D, **96**
    Class E, **96**
    summary, **97**
Classless Inter-Domain Routing (CIDR), 96, 253
CMD, for command prompt, 173
CNAME record, 206, 253
COMMAND, for command prompt, 173
communication
    connection-oriented, 56, 58, 253
    connectionless, 57, 61, 253
    peer-layer, 28, 256
computer names, 168
computer, viewing NetBIOS name of, 168
connection-oriented communication, 56, 58, 253
connectionless communication, 57, 61, 253
connections
    Session layer management of, 26
    testing, 48
contiguous bits, 142, 253
Crocker, Steve, 6

custom subnet mask, 133, **134–155**, 253
for Class A network, **148–149**
creation, **138–155**
network creation, **136**
rules, **137**
CuteFTP, 73, 253

D

damaged packets, 56
data base maintenance, for DNS, **202**
data flow control, ICMP (Internet Control
Message Protocol) for, **47–48**
Data-Link layer. *See also* Network
Interface layer
responsibilities of, **27**
data organization, in TCP (Transmission
Control Protocol), 60
data transfer across network, **9–11**
decimal numbering system, 36, 80, 253
converting binary to, **83**
converting to binary, **84–89**
using bit value method, **84–85**
using calculator, **88–89**
using division method, **86–87**
reviewing, **82**
default gateway, 40, 42, 128, 253
hardware address for, 41
specifying, 107
default subnet mask, 107
delivery guarantee, in TCP (Transmission
Control Protocol), 60
Department of Defense (DoD), 253
DHCP (Dynamic Host Configuration
Protocol), **109**
client release of IP address, 120
leases, **118–120**
setting duration, **122**
obtaining IP address from server,
110–117

process, 109
request searching for server, 62
reserving IP addresses, **121**
scopes and options, **123**
DHCP acknowledgment packet, **116–117**,
117, 253
DHCP discover packet, **110–111**, *111*, 253
DHCP offer packet, **112–113**, *113*, 253
DHCP request packet, **114–115**, *115*, 253
DHCP server, 108, 109, 253
diagnostics, ICMP (Internet Control
Message Protocol) for, **47–48**
directory, for HOSTS file, 174–175
division method, for decimal to binary
conversion, **86–87**
DNS (Domain Name Service), **176**, 253
on the Internet, **195**
name resolution using, **196–202**
what it is, **194**
DNS server, **203–207**
caching-only server, **205**
DNS zone transfer, **204**, *204*
primary name server, **203**
record types, **205–207**
secondary name server, **203**
DNS zone transfer, **204**, *204*
documentation, for Internet Protocol
version 6 (IPv6), **234**
DoD (Department of Defense), 253
DoD model, TCP/IP and, **29**
Domain Name Service (DNS). *See* DNS
(Domain Name Service)
domain name space, 195, 253
domains, 195, 253
dotted decimal notation, 90–91, 253
for subnet masks, 130
double-colon notation, 231, **232**, 254
duration of DHCP leases, setting, **122**
dynamic entry in ARP cache, 43

Dynamic Host Configuration Protocol
(DHCP), **109**
client release of IP address, 120
leases, **118–120**
setting duration, **122**
obtaining IP address from server,
110–117
process, 109
request searching for server, 62
reserving IP addresses, **121**
scopes and options, **123**

E

encapsulation, 20, 254
error messages, ICMP (Internet Control
Message Protocol) for, **47–48**
Ethernet, 20
Ethernet address, 36
exclusion of IP address from scope, 123,
254

F

failure recovery, as TCP/IP design goal, 8
fault tolerance, 254
secondary name server for, 203
File Transfer Protocol (FTP), **71–73**, 254
port for, 70
firewall, 48, 254
flexibility of TCP/IP, 3
FTP (File Transfer Protocol), **71–73**, 254
how it works, 72–73
port for, 70, 72
FTP command interpreter, 71, 73, 254
FTP command-line utility, 71, 254
user knowledge of commands, 73
FTP server, 254
FTP/TCP/IP, 72, 254
FTP Voyager, 73

G

gateway
default, 40, 42, 128, 253
hardware address for, 41
specifying, 107
GET request, 75
global option, 123, 254

H

handshake, three-way, **58–59**, 258
hardware
compatibility with TCP/IP, 2
NIC (network interface card), 36, 256
router, 40, 257
and IPv6 packets, 235
and IPv6 transition, 236
overloaded, 47
for packets to remote network, 128
reserving DHCP IP address for, 121
and subnets, 134
server. *See also* DNS server
for FTP, 71
NetBIOS name, 217
reserving DHCP IP address for, 121
Web, 69, 74, 259
standards, 20
TCP/IP independence from, 8
hardware address, **36–37**
broadcast to resolve, **44–45**
IP address resolution to, 43
TCP/IP determination of, **42**, *42*
headers in packets, 20, 254
for IPv6, 235
TCP vs. UDP, 63
hexadecimal numbering system, 36, 81,
254
for Internet Protocol version 6, **231**
home appliances, control through
Internet, 230

host name
    vs. NetBIOS name, 168
    query for, 207
host name resolution, **170–186**, 254
    broadcast, **180–181**
    cycle, **186**, *186*
    DNS (Domain Name Service), **176**
    HOSTS file, **174–175**
    LMHOSTS file, **182–183**
    local host (HOSTNAME), **172–173**
    NetBIOS name cache, **177–178**,
        184–185
    NetBIOS name resolution vs., **169**
    what it is, **167**
    WINS (Windows Internet Naming
        Service), **179**
Host record, 206
Host-to-Host layer, 56
HOSTNAME (local host), **172–173**, 254
hosts, 3, 18, 254
    for FTP, 71
    interaction with Network Interface
        Layer, 34
    IPv4 in IPv6 Internet, 236
    moving data streams to many, 49
    valid for Class C network, **152–155**
HOSTS file, **174–175**, 254
HOSTS.TXT file, 194, 254
HTML (Hypertext Markup Language), 74,
    75, 254
HTTP (Hypertext Transfer Protocol),
    74–75, 254
    port for, 70, 74
HTTP/TCP/IP packets, 74, 75, 254
hyperlinks, 74, 75, 254
Hypertext Markup Language (HTML), 74,
    75, 254
Hypertext Transfer Protocol (HTTP),
    74–75, 254
    port for, 70, 74

I

IANA (Internet Assigned Number
    Authority), 70, 255
ICMP (Internet Control Message
    Protocol), **47–48**
IETF (Internet Engineering Task Force), 6,
    255
IGMP (Internet Group Management
    Protocol), **49–51**
IN-ADDR.ARPA zone, 207, 255
incrementing number systems, 81
installing
    IP addresses, **102–109**
    TCP/IP on Windows 95/98, **104–105**
    TCP/IP on Windows NT, **102–103**
International Standards Organization
    (ISO), 20, 255
Internet
    DNS distribution across, 195
    origins, **4–5**
    TCP/IP and, 2
Internet Assigned Number Authority
    (IANA), 70, 255
Internet Control Message Protocol
    (ICMP), **47–48**
Internet Engineering Steering Group, 228
Internet Engineering Task Force (IETF), 6,
    255
Internet Group Management Protocol
    (IGMP), **49–51**
Internet layer in DoD model, 29, **36–37**,
    255
    ARP (Address Resolution Protocol),
        43–46
    ICMP (Internet Control Message
        Protocol), **47–48**
    IGMP (Internet Group Management
        Protocol), **49–51**
    Internet Protocol, **39–42**

Internet Protocol (IP), **39–42**
   determination of local or remote
     destination, **40–41**
Internet Protocol, Next Generation (IPng),
   228, 255
Internet Protocol version 4 (IPv4), 255
   need for new version, **228**
Internet Protocol version 5, 228
Internet Protocol version 6 (IPv6), 255
   addressing, **229–234**
   documentation, **234**
   hexadecimal addresses, **231**
   improvements of, **235**
   need for, **228**
   transition plan to, **236–237**
   Web site on, 267
Internet Service Providers (ISPs), TTL
   settings by, 122
internetwork, 12, 13, 255
Internetwork Packet
   Exchange/Sequenced Packet
   Exchange, 19
interoperability, of TCP/IP, 3
intranet, IP address reserved for, 93
inverse query, 207
IP addresses, 38, 255. *See also* name
   resolution
   automatic configuration. *See* DHCP
     (Dynamic Host Configuration
     Protocol)
   Class A, **92–93**
     standard subnet mask for, 132
   Class B, **94**
     standard subnet mask for, 132
   Class C, **95**
     standard subnet mask for, 132
   Class D, **96**
   Class E, **96**
   classes, summary, **97**
   converting version 4 to version 6, **233**
   determining host name for, 207

DHCP renewal, *118*, **120**
   dotted decimal notation for, **90–91**
   double-colon notation, 231, **232**
   installing and assigning, **102–109**
   in Internet Protocol version 6,
     229–234
     vs. version 4, **229**
   manual configuration, **105–108**
     and exclusion from DHCP scope,
      123
     for Windows 95/98, **108**
     for Windows NT, **106–107**
   obtaining from DHCP server, **110–117**
   reserved
     DHCP, **121**
     for IGMP packets, 49
     for private use, 93
   resolution to hardware address, 43
   subnetting rules, **137**
   version 4 within version 6 scheme,
     232
   version 6
     loopback address, **234**
     special, **234**
   what it is, **80**
IP (Internet Protocol), **39–42**
   determination of local or remote
     destination, **40–41**
IP Subnet Calculator, 135, *135*
IPX/SPX protocol suite, 19
ISO (International Standards
   Organization), 20, 255
ISPs (Internet Service Providers), TTL
   settings by, 122
iterative query, 200–201, 255

K

Kahn, Bob, 7

L

LAN Manager, 183, 255
layers in OSI reference model, 23, 255
  responsibilities of, **25–27**
leading zeros, in number conversion, 89
leases
  DHCP, **118–120**
    renewal, *118*
    setting duration, **122**
LLC (Logical Link Control), 27
LMHOSTS file, **182–183**, 188, 255
load balancing, 255
  secondary name server for, 203
local destination, IP (Internet Protocol)
  determination of, **40–41**
local host (HOSTNAME), **172–173**, 255
local IP address, subnet mask for finding,
  130–131
local network, 255
  identifying, **130–131**
logical address, 39, 255
Logical Link Control (LLC), 27
loopback address, 93, **234**, 255

M

MAC (Media Access Control) address, 36
MAC (Media Access Control) sublayer, 27
Mail eXchanger (MX) record, 207, 255
manufacturers, of network interface
  cards, ID number for, 36
Master DNS database, 255
  primary name server to contain, 203
Media Access Control (MAC) address, 36
Media Access Control (MAC) sublayer, 27
memory, for ARP cache, 43
Microsoft, overhead from ping-request
  packets, 48
Microsoft TCP/IP client, 177, 255

Microsoft TCP/IP Properties dialog box
  IP Address tab, *107*
    for subnet masks, *133*
  WINS Address tab, *178*
Multicast, 235, 255
multicast address, 49, 96, 255
MX record, 207, 255

N

nack (negative acknowledgment), 119,
  213, 218, 256
name registration
  with WINS, 179, **218–219**
  without WINS, 213, 216
name release request, 221
name resolution, 256. *See also* host
  name resolution; NetBIOS name
  resolution
  basics, **166–169**
  NetBIOS without WINS, **212–216**
  using DNS (Domain Name Service),
    196–202
    completing resolution, **200**
    data base maintenance, **202**
    querying DNS server, **197**
    querying name servers, **198–199**
    recursive and iterative queries,
      200–201
  with WINS, **217–221**
name server, 203, 256
Name Server (NS) record, 206, 256
NAT (Network Address Translation), 93,
  256
nbtstat command, 183–185, 256
NCP (Network Control Protocol), 4, 7,
  256
negative acknowledgment, 119, 213, 218,
  256
Net application (Microsoft), 168

NetBIOS, 256
  scope ID, 178
NetBIOS applications, **212–223**
  name resolution with WINS, **217–221**
  name resolution without WINS, **212–216**
  WINS manager, **222–223**
NetBIOS name cache, **177–178**, *184*, 214, 256
  displaying contents, **184–185**
  in host name resolution cycle, 188
  loading entries during boot process, 183
NetBIOS name query, 214, 256
NetBIOS name resolution, **187–189**, 256
  cycle, *188*, **188–89**
  vs. host name resolution, **169**
  what it is, **168**
NetBIOS name server, 217, 256
NetBIOS names, 256
  in LMHOSTS file, 182
NetWare, directory for HOSTS file, 175
network
  data transfer across, **9–11**
  identifying local or remote, **130–131**
  remote, 40
  topology, 34, 256
Network Address Translation (NAT), 93, 256
network administrator, 2, 256
Network Control Protocol (NCP), 4, 7, 256
Network dialog box (Windows 95/98), Configuration tab, *104, 108*
Network dialog box (Windows NT)
  Identification tab, *102, 106*
  Protocols tab, *106*
network interface card (NIC), 36, 256
Network Interface layer in DoD model, 29, **34–37**, 256

Network layer in OSI Model, responsibilities of, **26**
Network Neighborhood, 212
NIC (network interface card), 36, 256
Novell, protocol suite from, 19
NS record, 206, 256
NT Explorer, 168
numbering systems, 36, **80–89**
  binary, **82**
  converting binary to decimal, **83**
  converting decimal to binary, **84–89**
    using bit value method, **84–85**
    using calculator, **88–89**
    using division method, **86–87**
  decimal, **82**
  leading zeros and, 89

O

octal numbering system, 81
octet, 90, 256
open standard, TCP/IP as, 12
Open Standards Interconnection, 256. *See also* OSI reference model
operating systems, compatibility with TCP/IP, 2
OSI reference model, **23–28**, 256
  layer summary, **24**, *24*
  mnemonics to remember layers, 27
  responsibilities of layers, **25–27**
  use of, **28**
overhead
  from ping-request packets, 48
  of TCP/IP, 8

P

Packet InterNet Groper (Ping), 47, 257
packet-switched network, 256
  moving data on, **10**, *10*

packets, 10, 256
  acknowledgment of received, 26, 56, 58
  broadcast, 37
  damaged, 56
  DHCP acknowledgment, **116–117**, *117*
  DHCP discover, **110–111**, *111*
  DHCP offer, **112–113**, *113*
  DHCP request, **114–115**, *115*
  division into smaller, 60
  FTP/TCP/IP, 72
  hardware address for delivery, 37
  HTTP/TCP/IP, 74
  for IPv6, router treatment of, 235
  for name registration, 217
  Network Interface layer and, 35
  ping, *48*, **48**
  protocols to move, **20–21**
  sequence numbers for, 60
  TCP portion, *57*
  UDP portion, 57
parsing, 175, 256
password, for anonymous FTP, 71
peer-layer communication, 28, 256
physical address, 36
Physical layer in OSI Model, **27**
Ping (Packet InterNet Groper), 47, 257
  and host name resolution, 170–171
  packets, **48**, *48*
Pointer (PTR) record, 257
ports, **68–70**, 257
  for FTP, 72
  for UDP header, 61
  well-known, **70**
#PRE switch, 183
Presentation layer in OSI Model, responsibilities of, **26**
primary name server, **203**, 257
printers, reserving DHCP IP address for, 121
protocol stack, 2, 19, 257

protocol suite, 2, 19, 257
protocols, 2, 257
  ARP (Address Resolution Protocol), 42, **43–46**, 252
    broadcast for address resolution, **44–45**
  DHCP (Dynamic Host Configuration Protocol), **109**
    client release of IP address, 120
    leases, **118–120**, **122**
    obtaining IP address from server, **110–117**
    process, 109
    request searching for server, 62
    reserving IP addresses, **121**
    scopes and options, **123**
  FTP (File Transfer Protocol), **71–73**, 254
    how it works, 72–73
    port for, 70, 72
  HTTP (Hypertext Transfer Protocol), **74–75**, 254
    port for, 70, 74
  ICMP (Internet Control Message Protocol), **47–48**
  IGMP (Internet Group Management Protocol), **49–51**
  IP (Internet Protocol), **39–42**
    determination of local or remote destination, **40–41**
  IPng (Internet Protocol, Next Generation), 228, 255
  IPv4 (Internet Protocol) version 4, 255
    need for new version, **228**
  IPv5 (Internet Protocol version 5), 228
  IPv6 (Internet Protocol version 6), 255
    addressing, **229–234**
    documentation, **234**
    hexadecimal addresses, **231**
    improvements of, **235**
    need for, **228**
    transition plan to, **236–237**
    Web site on, 267

NCP (Network Control Protocol), 4, 7, 256

need for, **22**

SMTP (Simple Mail Transfer Protocol), 75

SNMP (Simple Network Management Protocol), 75

port for, 70

TCP (Transmission Control Protocol), 7, **58–60**, 258

data organization and delivery guarantee, **60**

header size vs. UDP, 63

three-way handshake, **58–59**, 258

TCP/IP (Transmission Control Protocol/Internet Protocol), 258

design goals, **8**

and DoD model, **29**

installing on Windows 95/98, **104–105**

installing on Windows NT, **102–103**

and name resolution, 166–167

origins, **7**

reasons to use, **12–13**

what it is, **2–3**

TFTP (Trivial File Transfer Protocol), 75

port for, 69, 70

UDP (User Datagram protocol), **61–63**, 258

for connectionless communication, 57

header size vs. TCP, 63

what they are, **18–21**

proxy server, 93, 257

PTR record, 207, 257

Q

query

iterative, 200–201, 255

NetBIOS name, 214

recursive, 200, 257

reverse, 207

R

radio on Internet, Class D address for, 96

RAM (random access memory), for ARP cache, 43

RAND Corporation, 4

read-only, 257

read-only copy of DNS database, 204

read/write, 257

read/write copy of database, 203

real-time, 257

real-time service, 235

records in DNS database, **205–207**

recursive query, 200, 257

redundancy, in ARPAnet, 5

registration

with WINS, 179, **218–219**

without WINS, 213, 216

reliability of communication, 56

remote IP address, subnet mask for finding, **131**

remote network, 40, 257

identifying, **130–131**

IP (Internet Protocol) determination of, **40–41**

remote resolution, secondary name server for, 203

Requests for Comments (RFCs). *See* RFCs (Requests for Comments)

reserved IP address, 257

for IGMP packets, 49

reserving DHCP IP addresses, **121**

resolve, 43, 257

resolver, 196, 257

reverse query, 207

RFCs (Requests for Comments), **6**, 257

1878 on subnet addressing, 137

801 on transition from NCP to TCP, 7

on Domain Name System, 194
on FTP, 71
for Internet Protocol, Next generation, 228
for Internet Protocol version 6 (IPv6), **234**
on IPv6 addressing, 234
for IPv6 transition, 236
Web sites for, **266–267**
for well-known ports, 70
root name servers, 197, 257
root of domain name space, 195
routability of TCP/IP, 3, 8, 12
router, 40, 257
and IPv6 packets, 235
and IPv6 transition, 236
overloaded, 47
for packets to remote network, 128
reserving DHCP IP address for, 121
and subnets, 134
routing, 38, 257
routing information
Network layer and, 26
in packet header, 20
routing table, 41, 257
RP record, 207

S

Scientific mode for calculator, *88*, 88
scope, 108, 109, 257
setting DHCP, **123**
scope ID, 178
scope option, 123, 257
secondary name server, **203**, 257
Select Network Component Type dialog box, 104, *104*
Select Network Protocol dialog box, 103, *103, 105*
sequence numbers, 60, 257

server. *See also* DNS server
for FTP, 71
NetBIOS name, 217
reserving DHCP IP address for, 121
Web, 69, 74, 259
server service, 212, 257
Session layer in OSI Model, responsibilities of, **26**
shares, 187, 258
Simple IPv6 Transition (SIT), 236, 258
Simple Mail Transfer Protocol (SMTP), 75
Simple Network Management Protocol (SNMP), 75
port for, 70
SIT (Simple IPv6 Transition), 236, 258
SMTP (Simple Mail Transfer Protocol), 75
SNMP (Simple Network Management Protocol), 75
port for, 70
SOA (Start of Authority) record, 206, 258
sockets, **68–70**, 258
software
standards, 20
TCP/IP independence from, 8
source IP address, 39
source-quench packet, 47, 258
SRI-NIC (Stanford Research Institute Network Information Center), 194, 258
standard subnet mask, **132–133**, 258
standards, need for, **22**
Stanford Research Institute, 5
Stanford Research Institute Network Information Center (SRI-NIC), 194, 258
Star Trek, Next Generation, 228
Start menu (Windows 95/98)
➢ Run, 173
➢ Settings ➢ Control Panel
➢ Network, 104, 108, 168
➢ Network ➢ Protocol ➢ TCP/IP, 170

Start menu (Windows NT)
➤ Programs ➤ Administrative Tools,
➤ WINS Manager, 222
➤ Run, 173
➤ Settings ➤ Control Panel
➤ Network, 102, 106, 168
➤ Network ➤ Protocol ➤ TCP/IP,
170
Start of Authority (SOA) record, 206, 258
static entry, 258
in ARP cache, 43
in WINS database, 222–223
stream, 49, 258
streaming audio and video, IGMP
(Internet Group Management
Protocol) for, **50–51**
subnet, 134, 258
subnet bits, 136, 258
rules for, 137
subnet calculator, 138, 258
Web sites for, 267
subnet goggles, 129, 258
subnet mask, 39, 258
custom, **134–155**, 253
network creation, **136**
rules, **137**
default, 107
standard, **132–133**
what it is, **128–131**
network and host, **129**
subnet mask creation, **138–155**
for Class A network, **148–149**
for Class B network, **150–151**
for Class C network, **154–155**
determining maximum number of
hosts, **140**
determining subnets needed, **139**
determining valid network addresses,
144–145
host IP addresses, range of valid,
146–147

mask determination
by calculation, **140–141**
using memorization or chart,
142–143
switches, 258
in LMHOSTS file, 183

T

target IP address, 39
TCP (Transmission Control Protocol), 7,
58–60, 258
data organization and delivery
guarantee, **60**
header size vs. UDP, 63
three-way handshake, **58–59**, 258
TCP/IP (Transmission Control
Protocol/Internet Protocol), 258. *See
also* Internet Protocol version 4 (IPv4)
design goals, **8**
and DoD model, **29**
installing on Windows 95/98,
104–105
installing on Windows NT, **102–103**
and name resolution, 166–167
origins, **7**
reasons to use, **12–13**
what it is, **2–3**
TCP/IP client (Microsoft), and name
resolution, 169
TCP/IP host, host name configuration,
170
TCP/IP Properties dialog box, 108
TCP/IP Setup dialog box, 103
testing, Class A IP address reserved for,
93
TFTP (Trivial File Transfer Protocol), 75
port for, 69, 70
three-way handshake, **58–59**, 258
Time To Live (TTL), 118, 258
setting duration, **122**

Token Ring, 20
Transmission Control Protocol/Internet Protocol). *See* TCP/IP (Transmission Control Protocol/Internet Protocol)
Transmission Control Protocol (TCP), 7, **58–60**, 258
 header size vs. UDP, 63
transmission error checks, by Session layer, 26
Transport layer, **26**, 29
 basics, **56–57**
 TCP (Transmission Control Protocol), **58–60**
 UDP (User Datagram protocol), **61–63**
Trivial File Transfer Protocol (TFTP), 75
 port for, 69, 70
troubleshooting
 HOSTNAME utility for, 173
 loopback address for, 234
TTL (Time To Live), 118, 258
 setting duration, **122**
TV on Internet, Class D address for, 96

U

UDP (User Datagram protocol), **61–63**, 258
 for connectionless communication, 57
 header size vs. TCP, 63
Unicast, 235, 258
Uniform Resource Locator (URL), 74, 258
 components, 176
United States Department of Defense, 4
 DoD model, **29**
University of California at Los Angeles, 5
University of California at Santa Barbara, 5
University of Utah, 5
Unix, directory for HOSTS file, 175
unspecified address, **234**

URL (Uniform Resource Locator), 74, 258
 components, 176
User Datagram protocol (UDP), **61–63**, 258
 header size vs. TCP, 63

V

vendor support, for TCP/IP, 3
video, sending streaming with IGMP, **50–51**

W

WAN connection, 259
 subnet address for, 138
Web browsers, 74, 259
Web servers, 74, 259
 port for, 69
Web sites
 connecting to, 74–75
 for RFCs, 6, 266–267
 for subnet calculators, 138
 for *TCP/IP Jumpstart*, **266–267**
well-known ports, **70**, 259
wide area networks, subnet address for connection, 138
Windows 95/98
 directory for HOSTS file, 175
 manually assigning IP address for, **108**
Windows Explorer, 168
Windows Internet Naming Service (WINS), 49, **179**, 259
Windows (Microsoft), Calculator, *88*, **88–89**
Windows NT
 directory for HOSTS file, 175
 installing TCP/IP on, **102–103**
 manually assigning IP address for, **106–107**

Windows NT Setup dialog box, 103, *103*
WINS (Windows Internet Naming
     Service), 49, **179**, 259
  in host name resolution cycle, 188
  name registration with, *218*, **218–219**
  NetBIOS name resolution without,
     212–216
  resources required by, 221
WINS Manager, *222*, **222–223**

WINS server
  IP address for, 217
  need for multiple, 221
WKS record, 207
workstation service, 212, 259

Z

zone file, 202
zone transfer, 204, *204*, 259

A+™ TEST PREPARATION FROM THE EXPERTS

Sybex presents the most comprehensive study guides for CompTIA's A+ exams for PC technicians.

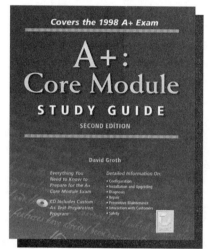

Covers the 1998 A+ Exam

A+: Core Module STUDY GUIDE
SECOND EDITION

David Groth

ISBN 0-7821-2344-9
800 pp. 7½" x 9" $49.99
Hardcover

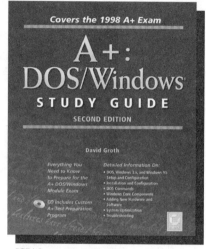

Covers the 1998 A+ Exam

A+: DOS/Windows STUDY GUIDE
SECOND EDITION

David Groth

ISBN 0-7821-2351-1
688 pp. 7½" x 9" $49.99
Hardcover

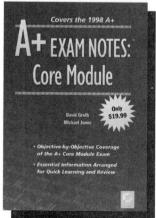

Covers the 1998 A+

A+ EXAM NOTES: Core Module

Only $19.99

David Groth
Michael Jones

• Objective-by-Objective Coverage of the A+ Core Module Exam
• Essential Information Arranged for Quick Learning and Review

ISBN 0-7821-2345-7
304 pp. 5⅞" x 8¼" $19.99
Softcover

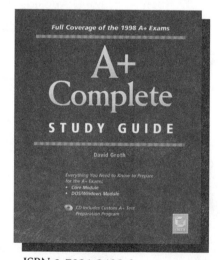

Full Coverage of the 1998 A+ Exams

A+ Complete STUDY GUIDE

David Groth

Everything You Need to Know to Prepare for the A+ Exams:
• Core Module
• DOS/Windows Module

ISBN 0-7821-2490-9
1104 pp. 7½" x 9" $49.99
Softcover

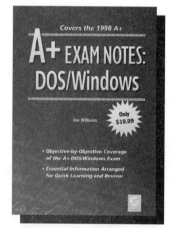

Covers the 1998 A+

A+ EXAM NOTES: DOS/Windows

Only $19.99

Jim Williams

• Objective-by-Objective Coverage of the A+ DOS/Windows Exam
• Essential Information Arranged for Quick Learning and Review

ISBN 0-7821-2346-5
304 pp. 5⅞" x 8¼" $19.99
Softcover

CompTIA.
One Industry. One Voice.

SYBEX
www.sybex.com

A+ Certification™
A CompTIA Certification Program

NETWORK+™ CERTIFICATION FROM NETWORK PRESS™

The Network+ certification from the Computing Technology Industry Association (CompTIA) is a vendor- and product-neutral exam intended to test and confirm the knowledge of networking technicians with 18–24 months experience.

Each Network+ book:
- *Provides full coverage of every CompTIA exam objective*
- *Written by experts who participated in the development of the Network+ certification program*